THE SCIENTIFIC LIVING SERIES

THE SEASONS PASS

THE HOW AND WHY SCIENCE BOOKS

by

GEORGE WILLARD FRASIER
HELEN DOLMAN
KATHRYNE VAN NOY

●

ILLUSTRATIONS

GUY BROWN WISER

●

COPYRIGHT, 1938 BY

THE L. W. SINGER COMPANY

SYRACUSE   CHICAGO   DALLAS

THE SEASONS PASS

2355.0

Back to School

"Jane! Are you ready?" called Nancy.

"I'm coming," answered Jane through an open window. "Wait just a minute."

It was the first day of school. Nancy had stopped for Jane.

Soon the girls were on their way. It was fun to be going to school again. The summer vacation was over. It had been a long vacation. In a few minutes the girls would be with their old school friends.

"Oh! there is Susan," cried Nancy. "Susan! Susan! Wait for us!"

Susan waited for Nancy and Jane and the three girls went to school together.

Bob and Jimmy had gone to school early. They were waiting for the girls at the school. A third boy was with them.

"This is Dick," said Bob to the girls. "He is going to be in our room this year."

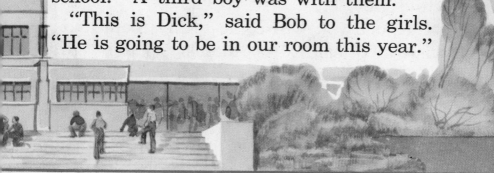

"We have a new teacher," said Jimmy. "Her name is Miss Parker."

"I hope she is nice," said Susan.

"My brother was in her room last year," said Bob. "He said she was the best teacher he ever had."

"She can't be any nicer than Miss Adams," said Jane. "I don't want to leave Miss Adams."

Soon the children were in their room. Miss Adams was there. The children gathered about her.

"Oh, Miss Adams," they cried. "Are you going to be our teacher?"

"Not this year," said Miss Adams. "I don't teach boys and girls who are as big as you are. I want you to meet your new teacher. Children, this is Miss Parker."

"Good morning, Miss Parker," said the children.

"I hope you will come to my room and visit me," said Miss Adams. "I must go now and meet my new children."

"Good-bye, Miss Adams," called the children. "Good-bye."

"Let's talk about vacations," said Miss Parker after she had learned the names of the children. "Tell me what you did this summer."

"I went to Uncle Ben's farm," said Jimmy. "I had a lot of fun. Uncle Ben has cows and sheep and many other animals. Guess how he gets water for them—with a windmill! A big windmill! When the wind blows, the windmill goes round and round. It makes the water come out of the pump. The windmill works for Uncle Ben.

"I got up early every morning. I helped Uncle Ben. I went to bed early, too. Uncle Ben said that getting up early and going to bed early would make me healthy. It

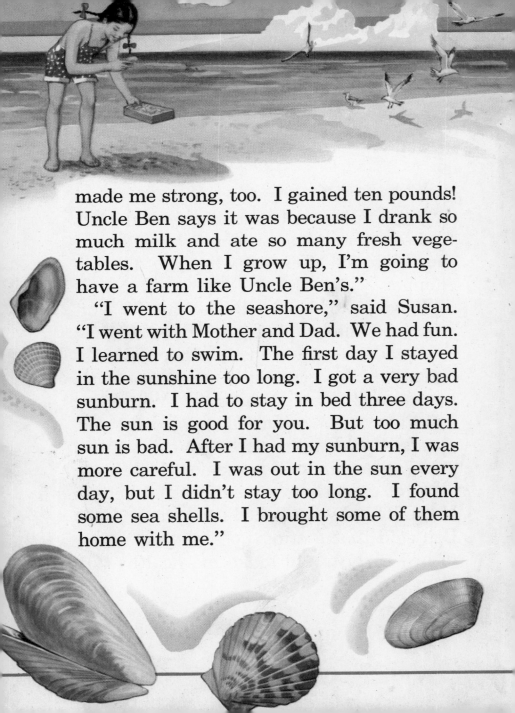

made me strong, too. I gained ten pounds! Uncle Ben says it was because I drank so much milk and ate so many fresh vegetables. When I grow up, I'm going to have a farm like Uncle Ben's."

"I went to the seashore," said Susan. "I went with Mother and Dad. We had fun. I learned to swim. The first day I stayed in the sunshine too long. I got a very bad sunburn. I had to stay in bed three days. The sun is good for you. But too much sun is bad. After I had my sunburn, I was more careful. I was out in the sun every day, but I didn't stay too long. I found some sea shells. I brought some of them home with me."

"I got sunburned, too," said Bob. "I
went to the mountains. The air was cool.
I wasn't a bit hot, but the sun burned me.
I found out that the sun can burn on a
cool day. We rode horseback. We caught
fish. I found a lot of rocks. I brought
back a box full of them. They are yellow
and brown and black and red and one is so
clear I can see through it. I want to go
to the mountains again next summer."

"I went to the mountains, too," said
Nancy. "I didn't get sunburned. I saw
some animals I had never seen before. I
saw some prairie dogs. They came out of
their holes. They sat up straight. Sometimes I could see a great many of them at

once. I saw a bear, too. It wasn't in a cage. It was in the woods. It was eating berries. It was a mother bear. She had two cubs. They were very funny. I took some pictures of them."

"My sister and I went to a camp," said Jane. "We were gone two weeks. The camp was on a lake. We learned to row a boat. We learned other things, too. We went on hikes. We went with a guide. He knew the name of every wild flower we found. We brought back many pictures of flowers. An art teacher showed us how to make pictures of flowers."

"I stayed home," said Dick. "I had a good time, too. Father and I watched birds every morning and night. Father bought me some field glasses. I could look through them at birds. I could see birds a long way off. I could look out of the window and watch birds in our yard. The field glasses made everything look bigger and closer. We saw twenty different kinds of birds in our yard. I know where there are fifteen different kinds of birds' nests. Some day I'll show you."

Next day the children brought their pictures and rocks and shells to school. They had a vacation show in the schoolroom.

A Trip to the Park

Ted and Joyce live in a big city. They live on the top floor of a big apartment house. When they look out of the window at the street below them, the people and cars look very small.

Ted and Joyce like the big city. They see many interesting things on the way to school. They like their school. When Ted and Joyce want to play out of doors, they go to the park. The park is not far from the apartment house. It has swings and seesaws and soft grass to play on. It has a zoo where many strange animals live.

Ted and Joyce are careful when they go across the streets. They watch for the green lights to go on. When the light across from them is green, it is safe to go across the street. Then the cars are stopped. Ted and Joyce are always careful when they go across the streets.

Uncle Don lives with Ted and Joyce. Uncle Don writes stories for children. Sometimes he goes to the park with Ted and Joyce. Then they have the most fun for Uncle Don is a very interesting man. He tells them stories. Sometimes they are make-believe stories; sometimes they are true stories. Ted and Joyce like the true ones better.

One afternoon in autumn, Uncle Don said, "Let's go to the park."

The children jumped up and the first thing Uncle Don knew, Ted and Joyce were pulling him to the door. Off they started for the park!

"Look!" said Joyce as they came near the park. "The park is beautiful. Some of the leaves are such pretty colors. They are turning red and yellow. I think autumn leaves are beautiful. Uncle Don, why do leaves turn red and yellow in autumn?"

"That's a long story," said Uncle Don. "But I can tell you part of it today. Come with me and we will look at a tree."

He led the children to an elm tree. Its leaves had not yet changed color. It was green. It was a beautiful tree.

"What a tall tree!" said Ted. "It must be as high as our apartment house!"

Uncle Don laughed. "Oh, no, it isn't that tall. But it is an old tree. This elm may be fifty years old."

"Really!" cried the children. "How can you tell?"

"I am just guessing," said Uncle Don. "I can't tell just how old it is. But it has such a large trunk that I think it must be an old tree. The tree keeps its same trunk and branches and roots year in and year out. The trunk grows larger around. The branches get longer. The roots grow deeper into the ground."

"What are roots?" asked Joyce.

"Roots are the parts of a tree that are under the ground," said Ted. "Once I saw a tree that the wind had torn out of the ground. The roots were big. There were almost as many roots as branches."

"Why does a tree have roots?" asked Joyce.

"Roots get water for the tree," Uncle Don told her. "Roots help a tree live."

"How?" asked Joyce.

"The roots spread out in the ground. Some of them are large. Some of them are small. The roots take up water that is in

the ground. You might say that the roots drink the water, but of course roots have no mouths. Roots can take in the water that is in the ground. The water goes through the roots and up into the tree trunk. It goes up the trunk just underneath the tree bark. The water travels into the branches and into the leaves. Do you know what this kind of tree has new every year?" asked Uncle Don.

"Leaves," said Ted.

"Yes, leaves and twigs," said Uncle Don. "Let's look at the leaves of the elm tree." He reached up to the tree and pulled off a leaf. "See the shape of the elm leaf. We call it a *simple* leaf because it does not have parts.

"The stems of the leaves are fastened to twigs. Here is an elm twig. See how the leaves are fastened to the twig.

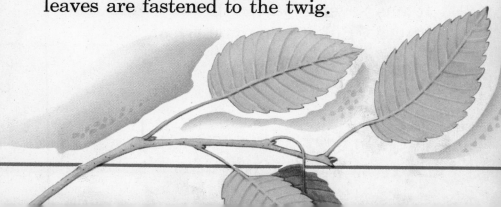

"Come with me and let's find a horse chestnut tree. I can show you some other things about twigs."

Not far away from the elm was a tree that had very large leaves.

"This is a horse chestnut tree," said Uncle Don, as he pulled off a leaf. "Look at its large leaf."

"It looks like several leaves on one stem," said Joyce.

"Yes, it does," said Uncle Don. "But what I have in my hand is one leaf. The horse chestnut leaf is not a simple leaf. It has several parts. It looks like many leaves. But it is only one leaf."

Uncle Don cut off a twig. "See how the stem of the leaf fits on the twig," he said. "And see this little bud."

The children looked at the twig. They could see the leaf stem and the bud. Ted pulled the leaf off the twig.

"Keep the leaf," said Uncle Don. "We will want to look at it later. Can you see the place where the leaf came off?"

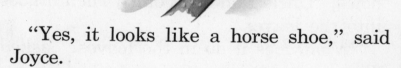

"Yes, it looks like a horse shoe," said Joyce.

"That's right," said Uncle Don. "We call that place a leaf scar."

"I can see some little dots on the leaf scar," said Ted. "They look like the holes in a horse shoe."

"Yes, they do," said Uncle Don. "Do you remember I said the water went up the trunk of the tree?"

"Yes," the children said.

"Then the water goes into the branches and into the twigs. It travels from the twig through the holes you see and goes into the leaf stem," said Uncle Don. "Let's look at the leaf that Ted has."

"There are holes in the leaf stem where it was fastened to the twig," said Ted.

"The water goes through these little holes," Uncle Don went on. "Then it goes into the leaves."

"What does it do in the leaves?" asked Joyce.

"The leaves use water in making food," said Uncle Don. "You see, trees must have food just as we do, but trees can't eat bread and butter! They use things that come from the ground and air to make their food. Food is made in the leaves. Sunshine helps the leaves make food. That is why plants need sunshine. The leaves work all day during the summer making food."

"How does the food get from the leaves to the rest of the tree?" asked Ted.

"The food travels back almost the same way the water comes up the tree," said Uncle Don. "The food is called sap."

"What happens to the sap?" asked Ted.

"A tree needs food just as you do. It uses some of the sap in growing. The food that isn't used is stored in the roots and branches. It will help keep the tree alive during the winter. Next spring the stored food will make the buds grow."

"I didn't know leaves were so important," said Joyce.

"It's time to go home now," said Uncle Don. "We'll come to the park together when the leaves have fallen off the trees. Then I can answer your question about why leaves change color."

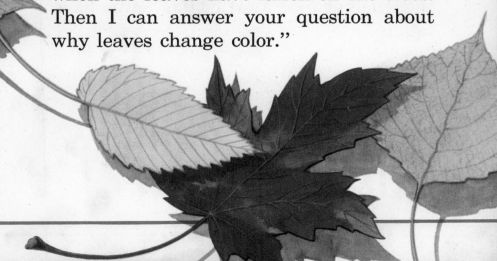

The Story of a Twig

Ted and Joyce watched every day for the leaves to fall off the trees. They liked to learn about trees from Uncle Don.

"Hurray! The leaves are falling!" shouted Ted one day when he came home from school. "Uncle Don, will you take us to the park?"

Uncle Don put down his glasses and laughed. "We're on our way!" he said.

This time Ted and Joyce had to wear their warm coats. The air was getting colder.

They went first to see the horse chestnut tree. "Oh!" cried Joyce. "It doesn't look the same at all. Most of the leaves have fallen."

Uncle Don cut off a twig.

"I see some buds," said Ted. "They did not fall off."

"No, these buds will grow into leaves and flowers next spring," said Uncle Don.

Joyce felt the buds. "They are sticky," she said.

"The sticky covering keeps the water from evaporating," Uncle Don told her. "If all the water evaporated during the winter, the bud would dry up. It could not grow when spring came."

"The buds have scales on them," said Ted.

"Yes," said Uncle Don. "Every bud has an outer covering of scales."

Uncle Don took off the outer scales. Underneath were some soft green scales.

Joyce felt them. "They feel soft. Will they grow into leaves next spring?"

"No," said Uncle Don. "The leaves are still inside these green scales." He pulled the green scales apart. Inside were the leaves. They were curled around a tiny stem.

"Some buds have only leaves. Some have only flowers. Sometimes there are both leaves and flowers in a bud. This bud has both leaves and flowers in it."

"Will the buds live through the winter?" asked Joyce.

"Yes, they will," answered Uncle Don. "Next spring they will swell. The scales will fall off and the leaves and flowers will come out."

"You said you'd tell us why leaves turn red and yellow in autumn," said Joyce.

"Oh, yes," said Uncle Don. He picked up the twig again. "See that leaf scar?"

The children nodded. "A covering has grown over it," said Ted.

"Yes, it has," said Uncle Don. "Something has grown between the leaf stem and the twig. Do you remember what you saw in the scar when you looked at it before?"

"There were little holes on the scar. The water came through the holes."

"That's right," said Uncle Don. "Now something has grown between the stem and the twig. It has covered up the holes."

"Then the water can't get through," said Ted. "And if the water can't get through to the leaves, the leaves can't make food for the tree."

"There you have the story," said Uncle Don. "When leaves can't get water, they die. When leaves are alive, they are green. When leaves die, they change color. Some turn red and some turn yellow."

"I think trees and leaves are very interesting," said Joyce.

"Twigs are interesting, too," said Uncle Don. "Each one tells a story of its age. Do you know that you can tell how old a twig is?"

"Tell us about it," said the children.

"Every leaf leaves a scar on the twig. The buds leave scars, too. The bud scars look like rings that go around the twig. If you count the bud scars on a twig you can tell how many years the twig has been growing. Here is a twig that is three years old. See. It has three bud scars."

"Let's play a game," said Joyce. "Let's see who can find the oldest twig."

Uncle Don played the game with the children. Each one found a twig. Each one counted the bud scars.

This was Ted's twig. How old was it?

This was Uncle Don's twig. How old was it?

This was Joyce's twig. How old was it?

"Can you tell the age of a tree, too?" asked Ted.

"Yes, but we would have to cut down a horse chestnut tree to tell how old it is," said Uncle Don. "We can tell how old an evergreen tree is without cutting it down. Let's find one and I'll show you."

Uncle Don and the children walked through the park looking for an evergreen tree.

"I see one," shouted Ted, and away he ran to an evergreen tree. "This is an evergreen tree," he said. "An evergreen tree keeps its leaves all winter. It is always green."

"Look at the shape of the evergreen tree," said Joyce. "It doesn't look like the horse chestnut tree at all. Its trunk is different."

"Its trunk goes all the way to the top of the tree," said Ted. "That's why it's different!"

The children looked up at the tree and its branches. Its trunk was straight and tall.

"Trunks of evergreen trees are used for telephone poles," said Uncle Don. "They are used for many things that need long, straight poles."

"Look at the way the branches come out of the trunk," said Ted. "They come out like this."

"The branches of the horse chestnut tree went like this," said Ted.

"That's right," said Uncle Don. "An evergreen branch grows out from the tree trunk. Several branches come out of the trunk near each other. They come out all around the trunk in a circle. Each year a new circle of branches grows out of the tree trunk.

"If you count the spaces between the branches all the way up the trunk, you can tell about how old the tree is."

Ted and Joyce counted. "There are twenty spaces," said Ted. "This tree must be about twenty years old."

"It must be," said Uncle Don.

"Where are the buds on an evergreen?" asked Joyce.

"They grow at the ends of the branches," Uncle Don answered. "Every year every branch has a bud on it. The bud opens and inside is a little bundle of needles. The needles are the leaves of an evergreen tree, you know. Every year the branches grow longer and longer."

"What makes the evergreen tree grow tall?" asked Joyce.

"On the tip of the tree trunk is a bud. Every spring the scales fall off and the bud opens. Inside it are leaves. Inside the leaves is a little stem. That is the way the tree trunk grows taller."

"The cones look like fruit," said Joyce "Are they?"

"Yes, they are," said Uncle Don. "Cones are the fruit of evergreen trees. They have seeds in them."

"Did you ever see the sap that comes from an evergreen?" asked Uncle Don.

"No," they cried. "Let's see it."

"The sap is the food of the tree," said Ted.

"You're right, Ted," said Uncle Don. "And the sap of evergreen trees sometimes comes out of the tree bark. When it comes out, it gets thick and sticky. See, here is some."

Uncle Don pulled off a little ball of sap. The children found some, too.

"M-m-m," said Joyce. "It smells good."

"Yes, and it tastes good," said Uncle Don. "Some people chew it like gum."

The children put some sap balls into their mouths. Ted liked the taste of the sap. But Joyce did not.

"I like the smell of it better than the taste," said Joyce. "Oh, Uncle Don! It's getting dark. We'll have to start for home."

"Yes, the days are getting shorter," said Uncle Don as they started for home. "Winter is coming."

The Life of a Butterfly

A female butterfly
lays eggs.

The eggs hatch.
Very small caterpillars
hatch out of the eggs.
The caterpillars eat
leaves. The cater-
pillars grow and grow.

Each caterpillar grows
too big for its skin.
It sheds its skin.
It has a new skin under-
neath the old skin.

The caterpillar grows
bigger and bigger.
Then it stops eating.
It moves slowly.

The caterpillar makes
a chrysalis. It rests
in the chrysalis.
We do not call it a
caterpillar now.
We call it a *pupa*.

The pupa changes to
a butterfly.
A butterfly comes out
of the chrysalis.

A female butterfly
mates with a male
butterfly.

The female butterfly
lays eggs.

This is the life of a butterfly.

The Birds Migrate

Autumn had come to Pleasant Valley.
The meadows were yellow with goldenrod.
The bushes and trees were turning red.

Squirrels were gathering nuts and putting them in trees. Chipmunks were running into their holes with their cheeks
full of seeds. Some animals were starting
to hibernate.

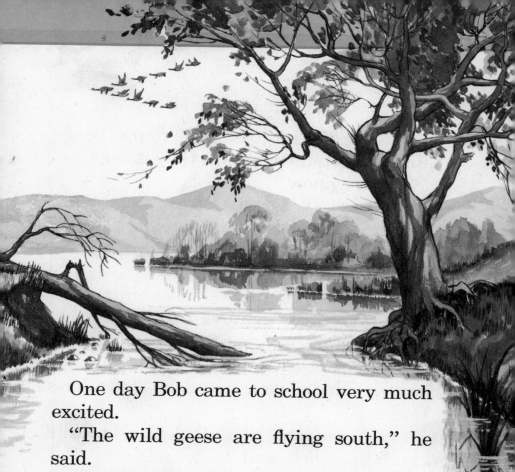

One day Bob came to school very much
excited.

"The wild geese are flying south," he
said.

"How do you know?" asked Susan.

"I heard them last night," said Bob.
"They made a funny noise. Dad says they
were honking."

"Like a car?" asked Jane.

"Well, no," said Bob. "Just something
like one. Dad says they are calling to
each other."

"Where did the geese come from?" asked Jimmy. "And where are they going?"

"I don't know," said Bob.

"Perhaps Dick can tell us," said Miss Parker. "He has been watching birds."

"I don't know about geese," said Dick. "But I'll ask Dad."

"Ask him where the blackbirds have gone, too. I saw many of them last week. Now they are all gone," said Jimmy.

"Perhaps Dick's father will come and answer some of your questions," said Miss Parker.

"Will you ask him, Dick?" asked the children. Dick said he would.

The next day Dick's father came to school with him. The children had some questions for him. Here they are.

1. Where do birds go in autumn?
2. Why do they go away?
3. Do they hibernate?
4. Why do some birds stay here all winter?

This is the story Dick's father told the children.

"For many years people have tried to answer these questions. Some people have watched birds for a long time. They know where some of the birds go, but they don't know why they go.

"The geese we heard were flying south. We say that they are *migrating*. Wild ducks are migrating now, too. Robins are migrating and so are blackbirds. Many birds are migrating in autumn.

"People used to think strange things about the migrating of birds. Some people thought birds hibernated like toads and frogs. But now we know that is not true. Some people thought birds flew to the moon! Do you know why birds couldn't fly to the moon?"

The children laughed. "It's too far," they said.

"Of course it is," said Dick's father. "But long ago people didn't know many things that we know today.

"Birds fly many, many miles to their winter homes. Most of them fly at night. That is why you heard the geese honking the other night. They were migrating.

"Most birds come together in flocks before they migrate. They do not go alone on the long trip south. Have you seen flocks of robins in your yards?"

"Yes," cried Jimmy. "There were a great many robins in our yard last night."

"They were getting ready to migrate," said Dick's father. "Male robins do not flock together in the summer. But in the autumn they gather in flocks before they migrate.

"The young robins flock together, too. They are as big as their parents in autumn, but they still have spots on their breasts. They usually migrate together. The females flock together, too, and go south."

"Some birds migrate before the robins. Orioles migrate before summer is over.

"Some day soon you may see the bushes in your yard full of birds. These birds have lived north of us during the summer. They are migrating and have stopped in your yard to eat. If your yard is a good feeding place, they may stay a while."

"Why do some birds migrate and some stay here all winter?" asked Jimmy.

"No one knows," said Dick's father. "People who study birds have some ideas about it, but they are not sure. Perhaps some day you may help to find the answer to that question."

"Thank you for coming and telling us about birds," said Miss Parker.

"Thank you very much," said the children.

Where Are the Frogs?

It was a holiday. The children had planned a picnic. They had invited their mothers and fathers. They had invited Miss Parker, too.

They went to the woods. The autumn sunshine was bright. They found a good place in the sunshine to eat their lunch. They sat on the ground near a pond.

"The woods are pretty," said Nancy.

"The leaves make them pretty," said Bob. "The leaves are different colors."

"There are only a few birds now," said Dick. "Most of them have migrated."

"The sunshine is bright but the air is cold," said Bob's mother. "I am glad we brought our coats. This is the last picnic we can have this year."

Bob and Jimmy ran down to the pond.

Jimmy put his hand in the water. "The water is cold," he cried.

"I don't see any frogs," said Bob.

"I don't think you will," smiled Miss Parker.

"Where are they?" asked Nancy.

"I wonder if you can guess," said Miss Parker.

"I bet they are hibernating," said Jimmy.

"Yes, they are, Jimmy," said Miss Parker. "Can you think of the place they would hibernate?"

The children thought but no one had an answer.

"If I gave you a pair of rubber boots and a spade, you might be able to find them," laughed Miss Parker.

"Oh," cried Jane. "Do they hibernate in the water?"

"Frogs couldn't hibernate in the water because they have to come up for air," said Susan. "They can't breathe in the water like fish and tadpoles can."

"That's right, Susan," said Bob. "Then they must hibernate in the mud."

"Good," said Miss Parker. "Good for you, Bob. They *do* hibernate in the mud."

"Well," said Dick. "I don't see how they could hibernate in the mud. They would still be under water. They couldn't get any air down in the mud."

Miss Parker laughed. "I'll tell you how they get air during the winter. They go down into the mud and dig holes. There is enough air in the holes to keep them alive all winter. They need very little air while they hibernate."

"Toads are very much like frogs," said Jimmy. "I haven't seen any toads in the garden this week. Are they hibernating?"

"Yes, they are," cried Dick. "Dad showed me a toad that was hibernating, didn't you, Dad?" He turned to his father.

"We were digging near the front porch and we almost cut the toad in two. Dad said it must have crawled under the front porch and dug down into the dirt. We found it sleeping in the hole it had made."

"Toads dig holes in dirt very much as frogs dig holes in mud," said Miss Parker.

"I like to look for animals," said Susan. "Let's look for some salamanders."

"I wonder who can find the first one," said Miss Parker.

Jane and Bob did not go on the hunt. The other children looked and looked, but they couldn't find any salamanders. Jane and Bob looked at Miss Parker and laughed. Soon they shouted, "You can't find any salamanders because they are hibernating!"

"How do you know?" the children asked as they came running back.

"We learned it last year," said Jane.

"I remember now," said Jimmy. "Salamanders hibernate in logs."

"That is right, Jimmy," said Miss Parker. "Salamanders often crawl inside old logs where the wood is dead and soft. They stay there until winter is over."

"Let's ask about snakes and lizards," said Jane. "Do they hibernate?"

"Yes," Miss Parker said. "Both snakes and lizards hibernate. They go under stones and rocks. Sometimes they go under logs. The garter snakes are about the last snakes to hibernate. They are also about the first ones to come out in the spring."

"This picnic has been fun," said Nancy's mother, "but now it is time to go home. The shadows are getting long. The sun goes down early now."

"We'll have to start getting ready for winter," Susan said.

"We fathers and mothers have learned some science," said Jimmy's father. "Perhaps you'll let us come to your science room some time and see your animals."

"We'd like to have you come," said Bob.

The children made the picnic place neat and clean. "We must leave it just as clean as we found it," said Jimmy.

"We won't need to leave food for the animals because they are hibernating," laughed Jane.

No Earthworms

Bob and Dick wanted to go fishing once more before winter. They had everything they needed but worms. They dug and dug but they couldn't find a worm!

"I wonder what has happened to them," said Dick. "We have always found worms right here. Last time we went fishing we dug a whole can full."

"Maybe we dug them all up," said Bob. "Or maybe the robins ate them."

"No, we didn't dig them all up," said Dick. "We left a great many of them last time. And I'm sure the robins didn't get them. Robins can't dig for worms. They get worms when the worms come to the top of the ground."

"Let's ask Miss Parker," said Bob. "Maybe she can tell us where the worms have gone."

"Oh! look, Bob," cried Dick. "There is something crawling on that piece of moss!"

"It looks like a snail," said Bob. "But snails live in water. We had some snails in our aquarium last year."

"Let's take it to school," said Dick. "I will put it in this can. Miss Parker will tell us what it is."

"Here are some more," cried Bob. "I can hardly see them. They look like the ground."

The boys put the snails into the can and took them to school. When they showed the snails to Miss Parker she said, "These are snails that live on land. We call them land snails."

"Let's put them into the aquarium," said Susan.

"No, we can't do that because they don't live in water," said Bob. "They are land snails. They live on land."

"How can we keep them if we don't put them into the aquarium?" asked Susan.

"We can keep them in this can," said Dick.

"I know a better place than the tin can," said Miss Parker. "We will make a home for them."

"How do you make a home for snails?" asked all the children at once.

"Didn't you make a home for your caterpillars last year?" asked Miss Parker.

"Oh, yes," cried the children. "We made homes for all our caterpillars."

"We put them in a glass box. We gave them food and took care of them," said Jane.

The children found a glass box. It was like the one they had used for their caterpillars.

"First we will need some stones and some dirt," said Miss Parker. "We will need some moss, too."

The children went to the woods to get these things. They put the stones in the bottom of the glass box. Then they covered the stones with dirt. They planted the moss in the dirt.

"Now we will put in a few small plants," said Miss Parker.

The children soon found some plants.

"Oh, look!" cried Susan. "There are some ants in our snail home. They were on the plants. Will the snails eat them?"

"No, snails will not eat ants," said Miss Parker.

"What can we feed the snails?" asked Jane.

"Snails will eat lettuce," Miss Parker told her. "We can get some at the store. We will feed the snails a little lettuce every day."

The children had fun making the snail home. They put in a few pretty rocks and some small pieces of wood. Jimmy found a small stick that looked like a log. He put it on the moss.

The children placed the snails in their new home. They put a glass top on the box.

"Do you know what we call this snail home?" Miss Parker asked.

"We called the fish home an aquarium," said Jane.

"Yes," said Miss Parker, "an aquarium has water in it. Fish live in it. Only animals that live in water can live in an aquarium.

"This is what we call the snail home." She wrote on the blackboard:

Terrarium

"A terrarium is a home for land animals. Only small animals that live on land can live in a terrarium."

"We have made a terrarium," said Jimmy. "Now we have a terrarium and an aquarium."

"Oh! We forgot to ask Miss Parker about the earthworms!" said Bob.

"Miss Parker, what has happened to the earthworms?" asked Dick. "We were digging for earthworms. We couldn't find any."

"Earthworms go down into the earth," said Miss Parker. "They stay all winter in the bottom of their holes. The colder it gets, the farther down they go."

"Earthworms hibernate!" said Bob. "We can't go fishing until next spring!"

A Surprise

One day Susan brought a box to school.
"I have a surprise for you," she told the
children. "I have it in this box."

"Is it an animal?" asked Jimmy.

"Yes," said Susan. "I found it in the
woods. Father said it was hibernating."

"Is it an earthworm?" asked Jane.

"Is it a snail?" asked Bob.

"No, it is not an earthworm, and it is
not a snail," said Susan. "It is an insect.
I found it in an old log."

The children were excited.

Nancy said, "Let me listen to it." She
listened but she couldn't hear a thing.

"Tell us more about it," said Dick.

"It has six legs," said Susan.

"We know it has six legs," said Jimmy.
"You said it was an insect. All insects
have six legs."

"It has four wings," said Susan. "I was
afraid to pick it up, but Father said it
was hibernating. There, I almost told you
what it is."

She opened the box. The children gathered around and looked into it.

"It's a bee. It's a bumblebee," said Jimmy. "It's sleeping."

"Didn't it sting you?" cried Nancy.

"Why was it in the log?" asked Bob.

"Were there other bees?" asked Jane.

Susan laughed at all the questions. "It was hibernating," she said. "Father said it would not sting when it was hibernating. It is a queen bumblebee. The queen lives all winter. The other bumblebees die. The queen finds a place to sleep. She stays there all winter. An old log is a good place for a queen bee to hibernate."

"Oh, it is moving," cried Jane.

"It is getting warm," said Miss Parker.

"What shall we do with it?" asked Susan.

Just then the bumblebee flew out of the box. It flew out of the open window.

Another Surprise

The next day Bob brought a box to school. He put it on the table. Then he wrote on the blackboard:

> There is an animal in the box.
> It has six legs.
> It has four wings.
> It is black and yellow.
> What is it?

"It's a bumblebee," cried Susan.

"No, it is not a bumblebee," said Bob.

"But, Bob, a bee is an animal," said Susan. "It has six legs and four wings. It is black and yellow. Your animal *must* be a bumblebee."

Bob only smiled.

"It's an insect," said Jimmy. "It has six legs."

"Does it sting?" asked Susan.

"Yes, it stings in the summer when it is not hibernating," said Bob.

"Is it a queen?" asked Jane.

"Yes, it is a queen," said Bob. He opened the box.

"How funny!" cried Susan. "It is an insect. It is black and yellow. It has four wings. But it doesn't look like a bumblebee. It is longer than a bumblebee and not so fat."

"This insect is a wasp," said Bob.

"It is hibernating," said Jimmy. "Where did you find it, Bob?"

"I found it under a board in the yard," said Bob. "Father told me it is a queen wasp."

"Yes," said Miss Parker. "It is a queen wasp. All the other wasps have died. The queens hibernate. Wasps and bumblebees are alike in many ways."

Other Insects That Hibernate

Miss Parker had a party for the children. They were eating ice cream.

"Ice cream is good," said Nancy. "I like ice cream."

"It will soon be winter," said Dick. "Then it will be too cold for ice cream."

"I like ice cream in winter just as well as in summer," said Nancy.

"There is an ant on the floor!" cried Susan. "I wonder if it eats ice cream."

"I don't think so," said Jimmy. "Ants store food in autumn. They couldn't store ice cream because ice cream melts."

"Do ants eat during the winter?" asked Bob. "Don't they hibernate?"

"We don't know," said Miss Parker. "We do know that ants go far down into the ground during winter. Many people have dug into ant hills in the winter. When it gets colder, the ants go so far down in the ground we can't find them."

"There is a fly!" cried Jane. "Look! It's going into a crack in the wall."

"Yes, that is where flies stay during the winter," said Miss Parker. "Some flies die before winter. The ones that live stay in cracks, or hide around pictures, or hide in any dark place."

"What other insects besides bees and wasps and ants and flies hibernate?" asked Jimmy.

"Some butterflies hibernate," said Miss Parker.

Susan was so surprised she almost dropped her ice cream. "I thought butterflies went south for the winter!" she cried.

"Just a few butterflies go south," said Miss Parker. "The Monarch butterfly goes south. Two kinds of butterflies live right here in our yards. Some butterflies live in the woods. Some die."

"Where do they live during the winter?" asked Bob.

"Sometimes they live under boards," replied Miss Parker. "Those that stay in the woods live under the bark of trees."

The Snails

Miss Parker came to school early one morning. She looked at the terrarium. Something had happened. She lifted off the glass cover and looked inside. Then she placed the cover on the top again. She wrote this sentence on the board:

The snails won't need any lettuce today.

The children soon arrived. Nancy was the first to see the sentence. She began to wonder. She looked at the terrarium. Soon everyone had read the sentence. The children were all looking at the terrarium.

Jimmy came up last and looked in.

"Oh," he said, "I see . . ."

"Don't tell," said Miss Parker. "Let's see if we can all find out."

After everyone had looked into the terrarium, Miss Parker said, "Now tell us what you saw. You looked first, Nancy. You may tell first."

"I didn't see anything," said Nancy. "I couldn't even see the snails."

"I couldn't see them either," said Bob.

"I saw the snails under a piece of wood," said Jimmy.

Nancy looked again to see if Jimmy was right. "Yes, there they are," she said. "Are they hibernating?"

"Yes," said Miss Parker. "Lift them out, Nancy. Let's look at them."

Nancy picked up one of the snails carefully. She held it in her hand.

All the children looked at it.

"I see something new," said Jane. "The opening in the shell is closed."

"Do you remember the little tracks or trails we saw on the glass of the terrarium last week?" asked Miss Parker. "The same kind of material closes the opening of the snail shell."

"Why is the opening closed?" asked Jimmy.

"It protects the snail while it is hibernating," said Dick.

"What do you mean, Dick, when you say *protects?*" asked Miss Parker.

"Well, insects can't crawl in. Water can't get in. It keeps out dirt, too," said Dick.

"Many animals are hibernating," said Nancy. "None of them will eat until next spring."

"I'm glad I'm not going to hibernate," said Bob. "I like to eat."

The children laughed.

Jimmy wrote the names of all the animals he could remember that hibernate. These are the names he wrote.

queen bumblebee	frog
queen wasp	toad
salamander	fly
lizard	earthworm
garter snake	woodchuck

Do you know the name of any animal that Jimmy forgot?

Four Friends

With eyes	I see
nose	smell
mouth	taste
and	and
ears	hear

Ted wrote this on the blackboard at school. Right under it he wrote:

Our eyes, nose, mouth, and ears
are our four best friends.

Yes, Ted is right. Our eyes, nose, mouth, and ears are our best friends.

Eyes

We see with our eyes. Without them all of the world would be dark. We could not see the faces of our schoolmates. We could not see the flowers or birds. Yes, our eyes are our good friends.

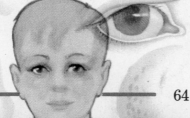

Each eye has two eyelids. When these lids are closed, we can not see. The lids can close very quickly. They keep things from getting into our eyes. They are closed when we are asleep.

Look at your eyes in a mirror. Can you see hairs on the edge of the lids? We call them eyelashes. They, too, help keep things from getting into our eyes.

If something gets in your eye, do not rub your eye. Tears will come and wash out the dirt. If the tears do not wash out the dirt, go to a doctor or a nurse. If you rub your eye it will be very sore.

When you read, have the light behind you. Sit so the light will come over your shoulder.

When the sun is bright, wear a hat. Then the sunlight will not hurt your eyes.

Some boys and girls need glasses. Glasses help to make weak eyes strong. Your doctor will tell you if you need them. If you have glasses, wear them. Always keep your glasses clean.

Take good care of your eyes.

Nose

You know what your nose does for you. It helps you smell. Think of the fun it gives you. When Mother is getting dinner, you like to smell the good things she is cooking. You like to smell flowers in the garden.

Did you know that smell makes food taste better? When you have a bad cold and you can not smell, food does not taste good. Hold your nose when you eat something and see what happens. Mother tells you to hold your nose when you take bad medicine. Why? Because the medicine doesn't taste so bad when you can't smell it.

Look in the mirror. See the two holes in your nose. You breathe through them. Air goes into your body through them.

You may be able to see some little hairs in these holes. The hairs help keep dust out of your nose. They help make the air you breathe clean. Your nose also warms the air that goes into your body.

You must remember some things about your nose. Here are six of them:

1. Always keep your nose clean.
2. Blow your nose on a clean handkerchief or on a paper handkerchief.
3. Never use another child's handkerchief when you blow your nose.
4. Never pick your nose.
5. Never put anything into your nose.
6. There is a right way to blow your nose. Ask the doctor or the nurse to show you.

Your nose is one of your four best friends. Take good care of it.

Mouth

You eat and drink through your mouth. You taste things in your mouth. Sometimes you breathe through your mouth. But this is not a good way to breathe. You have hairs in your nose to keep dust out when you breathe. You have no hairs in your mouth. Your nose warms the air you breathe. Your mouth does not warm the air. So your body gets clean warm air if you breathe through your nose.

Breathe through your nose and let your mouth eat, drink, talk, and taste.

When food goes into your mouth, you taste it. You must also chew it. Food should be chewed many times. Then it

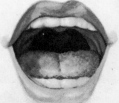

goes down into your stomach. If you eat too fast and don't chew your food well, you may have a stomach ache! You should also drink water and milk.

Your mouth helps you talk. Your teeth, tongue, and lips all help. Look in the mirror. Talk. See how your tongue moves. See how your lips help make words.

Keep your mouth clean. How do you do that? Not with soap and water. You must keep your mouth shut. If you go around with your mouth open, you will get dirt in it.

Never put anything but food and drink into your mouth. Some children put pencils into their mouths. Some put toys and even pennies into their mouths. Some big boys and girls do it, too. But they should not. They might get diseases from the people who have handled these things.

Keep your teeth clean. Clean them with a toothbrush. Clean between them with dental floss.

Your mouth is one of your best friends. Take good care of it.

Ears

This friend helps you hear. The part that hears is inside your head. The sound you hear goes in through the hole you can see when you look in your mirror.

The ear works best when it is clean. Wash your ears with a soft cloth on the end of a finger. Never dig your ears. Never put anything into them. If you have earache, you should go to the doctor.

Ears are very useful. Without them you could not hear. Take good care of them.

A Nest Hunt

One day Dick brought something new to school. It was in a box. The children wanted to know what it was.

"Guess," said Dick.

"Is it alive?" asked Susan.

"No," said Dick. "But something alive made it."

"Did an animal make it?" asked Bob.

"Yes," said Dick. "An animal that didn't have any hands made it."

"Tell us more about it, Dick," said Miss Parker.

"Well, it was once an animal's home. It is made of grass. Four little . . . Oh! I almost told!"

"Oh, I know," shouted Jimmy. "It's a bird's nest."

"That's right," said Dick as he opened the box and showed a nest to the children.

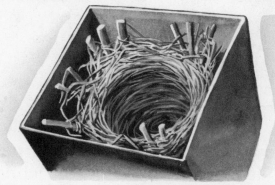

"What kind is it?" asked Nancy.

"A red-winged blackbird made it," said Dick.

"Where did you find it?" asked Bob.

"When Dad and I were at the lake last summer, we watched red-winged black-birds. They were in the weeds at the edge of the lake. One day we saw a red-winged blackbird carrying an insect. Dad thought we might find a nest. We got in the boat and rowed into the weeds. We could see a nest but we didn't get close to it. The male bird made a lot of noise. He was so excited that we left.

"Yesterday we were at the lake again. The birds were all gone. So we rowed out and got the nest."

"Now the birds won't have a home next year," said Nancy.

"Birds don't use their nests after the young birds are grown," said Miss Parker. "There is no harm in taking nests now."

"See how this nest is woven around the stems of the weeds," said Jimmy.

"It is a deep, firm nest," said Miss Parker. "Not all birds make such good nests."

"I know where there is a nest that you can see through," said Jimmy.

"I know where there is a nest made of mud," said Bob.

"Would you like to go on a nest hunting trip?" asked Miss Parker. "Dick may lead the way. Perhaps we'll see some other nests, too."

All of the children looked for nests as they walked along. They looked in bushes. They looked in the trees. The leaves were gone and it was easy to see the nests.

"I see a nest!" said Miss Parker.

"Where?" asked the children. They were looking up at a tree.

"It isn't in the branches," said Miss Parker.

"Do you mean that hole?" said Jane.

There was a hole in the tree trunk about as high as Miss Parker's head.

"Is that a woodpecker's nest?" asked Susan.

"I think so," said Miss Parker.

The hole was round. "The nest is at the bottom of the hole," said Miss Parker. "The bird lays her eggs in there."

The children walked on and Jimmy found the nest he had talked about.

"Look, you can see through it," he said.

The nest was on the branch of a spruce tree. It was made of some sticks laid across each other.

"What kind is it?" asked Jane.

"It is a mourning dove's nest," said Miss Parker.

"It doesn't look like a very good nest," said Nancy. "Wouldn't the eggs roll out?"

"A mourning dove lays only two eggs," said Miss Parker. "The eggs almost never roll out of the nest."

Bob was leading the way to the mud nest he had told about.

Suddenly Nancy stopped. "I see a nest!" she cried.

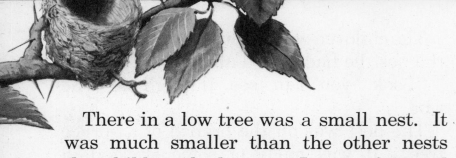

There in a low tree was a small nest. It was much smaller than the other nests the children had seen. It was fastened between two little branches.

Miss Parker reached up and got the nest. She gave it to Nancy.

"How soft it is!" said Nancy.

"How thick the sides are!" said Jane.

"It's like a cup," said Susan. "What kind is it, Miss Parker?"

"I think this is a goldfinch's nest. Let me look to be sure." Miss Parker looked at the inside of the nest.

"Yes, it is," she said. "It is lined with thistledown. Goldfinches make their nests about the time thistles are ripe and they use the soft thistledown to line their nests."

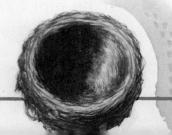

"We saw goldfinches on the thistles last year," said Bob.

"Goldfinches like to eat thistle seeds," said Miss Parker. "Some people call them thistlebirds."

"This is a good nest," said Nancy. "The eggs wouldn't fall out of this nest."

The children walked on.

"Here is my house," said Bob. He led the way to the garage and pointed up toward the roof.

"I don't see anything," said Jane.

"Oh, I do," said Jimmy. "Up under the edge of the roof."

A mud nest was stuck against the side of the garage.

"If Dick will help me bring a ladder, we can get the nest," said Bob.

The boys found a ladder and put it against the side of the garage. Jimmy and Dick held the ladder while Bob climbed up and got the nest.

The nest was made of mud with some horse hairs sticking out of it. It was lined with feathers. The side that had been stuck against the garage was flat. The other side was rounded.

"I know what kind of bird made this," said Bob. "Dad and I saw her making it. Dad said these birds often build in barns."

"What bird made it?" asked Susan.

"A barn swallow," said Bob. "I saw the female carrying mud in her mouth. She stuck it to the side of the garage. She was a long time building the nest."

"Did you watch the birds after the nest was finished?" asked Dick.

"Yes, I watched them every day until the baby birds were ready to fly. One day I saw the baby birds on that wire near the nest. The mother and father birds were feeding them. The baby birds would open their mouths and make funny noises. The mother and father would fly down. They would drop food into the baby birds' mouths as they flew by."

"You've had a good chance to watch, Bob," said Miss Parker. "Haven't you learned interesting things about many birds?" she asked the children.

"Oh, yes!" the children cried.

"Different birds make different kinds of nests," said Susan.

"They're like people," said Jimmy. "Some people make houses of brick and some use wood. Some birds make their nests of mud and some use sticks. Some use grass and some use thistledown."

"But the same kind of birds usually make the same kind of nest," said Miss Parker.

"That's right," said Dick. "A robin's nest always has mud and grass in it."

Taking the Cattle to Market

"I think we had better take our cattle to market," said Jack's father.

He was looking at the cattle in the feeding pen. Cowboy Hal and Jack were with him.

"Yes, they are ready," said Cowboy Hal.

"How do you know when cattle are ready for market?" asked Jack.

"We watch them every day," Cowboy Hal said. "When we brought them in from the summer pasture, they were not ready. So we have been feeding them again. Now see how broad their backs are. They are not too fat. They are solid. They were not broad and solid like this when we brought them in from the pasture. See how thick their legs are. Their necks are short and thick, too. These cattle will make very good beef. Yes, they are ready for market."

"We will sell them tomorrow," said Father to Cowboy Hal. "You and Jack may drive them to market."

Early next morning Cowboy Hal and Jack started for the market. They rode their horses. But they rode very slowly.

"We must not drive cattle fast," said Cowboy Hal. "They are too fat to run."

"Why do they have such thick hair?" asked Jack as they rode along.

"The hair of most animals gets thicker in autumn," said Cowboy Hal. "Their thick hair will keep the heat in their bodies. Their thick hair keeps them warm in winter."

"They need thick hair when the days get cold," said Jack. "Most of our cattle stay out in the fields in winter. They don't have sheds to go into when it's cold."

"Will these cattle be made into beef?" asked Jack.

"Yes," said Cowboy Hal. "And they will make very good beef."

"Why don't we sell all our cattle?" asked Jack.

"Some are not old enough to sell," said Cowboy Hal. "We keep others so we can have milk."

"That's good," said Jack. "I like milk."

"Milk is good for you," said Cowboy Hal. "The cows we milk do not look like the cattle we sell for beef. They are never as solid as beef cattle. Some cows give us very good milk. Cows should have clean places in which to live. They should have plenty of food to eat and good clean

water to drink. They should be kept in barns when it is very cold."

"There is another reason why we do not sell all our cattle," said Cowboy Hal. "Can you guess what it is?"

"Oh, yes!" said Jack. "We must keep some of them or we couldn't have more next year. The cows will have babies."

"That's right," said Cowboy Hal. "But if you want to be a real cowboy call them calves and not babies."

"All right," said Jack. "But they are like babies. They are born alive."

"Yes, and the mother cow feeds her calf milk," said Cowboy Hal. "You were born alive and your mother fed you milk."

Jack liked to go to market. He hoped he could go again next year.

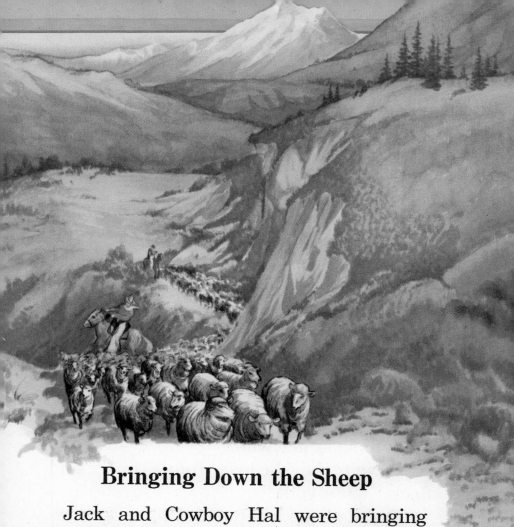

Bringing Down the Sheep

Jack and Cowboy Hal were bringing down the sheep from the mountains. The sheep had been eating in the mountains all summer.

"They are fat," said Jack. "And their wool is thick on their backs."

"Yes, a sheep's wool gets thicker in autumn. It will keep the heat in the sheep's body this winter." said Cowboy Hal. "Wool keeps the sheep warm."

"A sheep has to keep warm," said Jack. "It stays out of doors all winter."

"Its skin is thick, too," said Cowboy Hal. "The thick skin helps keep it warm. A sheep is well protected for winter. Say, what's the matter with that sheep's mouth? It must be cut."

Cowboy Hal jumped off his horse and ran to a sheep. Jack jumped off his horse, too. The sheep's mouth had blood on it.

"It isn't a bad cut," said Cowboy Hal, looking at the sheep's mouth carefully. "It will soon get well."

"Hasn't the sheep a funny lip?" said Jack. "It's split."

"Yes, a sheep has a split lip," said Cowboy Hal.

Jack looked again at the sheep's mouth. "It hasn't any teeth," he said.

Cowboy Hal laughed. "Oh, yes, it has. Look at the lower jaw. It has sharp cutting teeth in front and grinding teeth in the back. It doesn't have any teeth in its front upper jaw. But it does have grinding teeth in its back upper jaw."

"Sheep have hard gums and strong lips," said Cowboy Hal. "Their tongues are strong, too. Sheep can eat grass that other animals can't get. They can cut grass almost down to the roots."

"How do they do it?" asked Jack.

"A sheep twists its tongue around some grass. Its tongue is so strong that it breaks off the grass."

"Do they twist their tongues around mountain grass?" asked Jack.

"Yes, we raise sheep in the mountains because they can eat the short grass that grows between rocks. Sheep can cut almost all the grass on a mountain side. They don't leave any grass for the cattle to eat. Many ranch people do not like to raise sheep. They say that the sheep eat all the good grass."

"Why does Father raise both sheep and cattle?" asked Jack.

"He has so much land that he has room for both sheep and cattle," said Cowboy Hal. "He lets the cattle eat on the meadows. He lets the sheep eat on the mountain sides."

"I know why sheep can live on mountain sides," said Jack. "They have little feet. They have strong legs, too."

"Yes, they do have little feet and strong legs," said Cowboy Hal. "Have you ever noticed their small hoofs?"

"Yes, their hoofs are split," said Jack.

"Their hoofs are really two toes," said Cowboy Hal. "Cows and goats have split hoofs, too."

Sheep's hoof   Cow's hoof   Goat's hoof

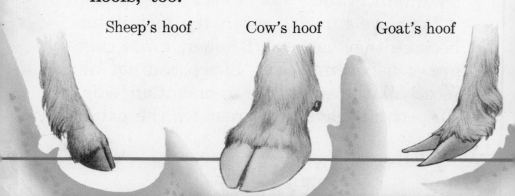

"Mountain goats must have small hoofs," said Jack. "I've seen them run up mountain sides."

"Even tame goats can climb mountains," said Cowboy Hal. "Many people keep goats. They use the goats' milk."

"Do they drink it?" asked Jack.

"Oh, yes, it is very good. Many people like it better than cows' milk. Goats' milk can be made into butter and cheese just as cows' milk can."

"Do baby goats get milk from their mothers?" asked Jack.

"Yes, sheep and goats and cows all feed their young on milk."

"Do goats have wool?" asked Jack.

"No, they have hair. In autumn it gets

thick. It keeps them warm during the winter. In spring it can be cut off. Goats' hair is used to make many fine clothes. It is softer than wool. It is almost as warm as wool."

"Cows and goats and sheep have split hoofs and they all feed their young on milk," said Jack. "Are they alike in any other way?"

"Yes, indeed," said Cowboy Hal. "They all chew cuds!"

Jack laughed. "That's right, they do. But I want to know what a cud is."

Cowboy Hal told him, "Cows and goats and sheep are called cud-chewing animals. Their stomachs are not like the stomachs of most other animals. Their stomachs have parts in them. Have you seen a cow chew her cud?"

Of course Jack had! "She chews her cud from side to side like this." Jack moved his mouth and lips from right to left.

"A sheep does the same thing," said Cowboy Hal. "A sheep cuts and swallows the grass as fast as it can. It does not take time to chew the grass as it cuts. The grass goes to one part of the stomach and is made into small balls. When the sheep has finished eating, it lies down. It brings up one of the balls of grass and chews for a long time. Then it swallows the grass. This time the grass goes to another part of the stomach. The sheep brings up another ball and chews that. We say that the sheep is chewing its cud.

"Cows and sheep and goats are alike in another way," Cowboy Hal went on. "Their teeth are alike. They all have grinding teeth but they do not have cutting teeth in their front upper jaws. They have to use their tongues in getting their food."

The Deer

"Oh, Jack, I see another cud-chewing animal," said Cowboy Hal. He pointed toward some trees near the lake. Jack looked but he couldn't see the animal.

"Look again," said Cowboy Hal. "If you look closely, you will see a deer."

Jack looked again. "Oh, now I see it," he laughed. "It looks so much like the ground and the trees I can hardly see it. Did you say a deer chews a cud?"

"Yes, a deer chews its cud. It is like the cow and the sheep and the goat. It chews a cud. It has no upper front teeth. It has small hoofs. Its young are born alive and it feeds its young milk."

Jack got off his horse and walked toward the deer. But the deer ran away.

"The deer has a thick coat of hair," said Jack when he got back to Cowboy Hal. "The deer stays in the woods all winter. I guess its thick coat of hair will have to keep it warm this winter. The deer has no barn or shed to stay in."

These animals are cud-chewing animals.

They have no front upper teeth.

They have hoofs.

Their young are born alive.

They feed their young on milk.

Their hair or wool is thicker in winter.

Taking Care of Rat Tail

"Does the hair of all animals grow thicker in autumn?" asked Jack.

"The hair of most animals grows thicker," said Cowboy Hal. "Look at Rat Tail. His hair is already getting thicker."

Jack looked at his horse. "Yes, his hair is thicker now than it was last summer. Rat Tail won't be cold this winter."

Jack knows how to take care of Rat Tail. He feeds Rat Tail hay every day. He feeds Rat Tail oats and corn.

Jack always lets Rat Tail rest after eating. Horses should not be ridden too soon after they eat. They should rest for a while. Children should rest after eating, too.

Jack brushes and combs Rat Tail's hair almost every day.

In winter when Rat Tail is hot from running, Jack covers him with a blanket. This keeps Rat Tail from taking cold. Horses can get colds. Sometimes they get very sick.

When animals on the ranch get sick, Jack's father sends for a doctor. This doctor takes care of animals. He gives medicine to horses and cows and sheep. Sometimes he puts the sick animals in a pen where no other animals can get near them. Then the other animals will not get sick.

Jack does not want Rat Tail to get sick. He takes good care of Rat Tail.

Jack's Teeth

Jack told his mother all he had learned from Cowboy Hal. "Cattle and sheep are very interesting, Mother. And goats are, too. I'd like to know more about them."

"Yes, cattle and sheep are very interesting," said Mother. "But so are boys and girls. I could tell you a great many interesting things about yourself."

"Oh, please do," said Jack.

"Then let's begin with your teeth," said Mother. "You have three kinds of teeth. In the front you have four cutting teeth on your lower jaw and four cutting teeth on your upper jaw."

Jack looked in the mirror.

"I see them," he said. "The sheep had cutting teeth on its lower jaw. But it had no cutting teeth on its upper jaw."

"Then you can cut food better than a sheep," said Mother. "Right next to your cutting teeth you have tearing teeth."

"One on each side makes four," said Jack. "Yes, I can see all four of them."

"Your other teeth are grinding teeth," said Mother. "You use them when you chew food.

"When you were a baby, you had no teeth. Here is a picture of you when you were three months old. See, no teeth!

Then you had to live on milk and orange juice and very soft food. No meat or vegetables for you then.

"This picture," Mother went on, "was taken when you were two years old.

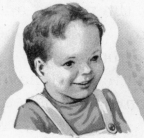

"See, you had some teeth. Those were baby teeth. You had twenty baby teeth.

Eight of them were cutting teeth, four were tearing teeth, and eight were grinding teeth. You have lost all of them now. Some of them came out easily. Some of them were pulled out by the dentist.

"This is a funny picture," said Mother. "It was taken when you were seven years old. You had lost some of your front baby teeth. Your new teeth had not grown in."

Jack looked at the picture and laughed. He did look funny. But now he had new cutting teeth in front.

"How many teeth will I have when all my new teeth come in?" asked Jack.

"Twenty-eight or thirty-two," said Mother. "Most people have thirty-two teeth, but some have only twenty-eight.

People who have only twenty-eight teeth have eight cutters and four tearers in front but only sixteen grinders.

"Your teeth are straight," Mother went on. "But some children have crooked teeth. Then the dentist has to put wires on them to make them straight."

"I know how to take care of my teeth," said Jack. "I learned in school. I keep them clean by brushing them. I always brush them up and down. I use dental floss, too. I break off a piece. I put it around a finger on each hand. Then I pull it between my teeth. No food can stay between my teeth when I use dental floss. I go to the dentist if I have a toothache. Do you think my teeth will last a long time?"

"Oh, yes, I think you will have them a long time. You keep them clean. You never bite anything that is hard. I think they will work for you for many years."

"I thought the sheep's teeth were interesting," said Jack. "But I think mine are much more interesting."

High in the Mountains

"Wake up, Jack!" called Cowboy Hal one morning. "The oatmeal is done. The eggs will soon be ready."

"I'd rather sleep," said Jack.

"Too bad!" said Cowboy Hal. "Then I'll be all alone on that mountain trail today."

"Mountain trail!" cried Jack. "I'll be at the table before the eggs are done!" And Jack was there!

"I guess I was hungry," said Jack. "I like breakfast. I like oatmeal and eggs and milk."

"You need a good breakfast," replied Cowboy Hal. "You'll need lots of strength today. Good food gives you strength. You can't climb mountains without food."

The horses were ready and away they went.

"The shadows are long this morning," said Jack.

"Yes, the sun is not very high," said Cowboy Hal.

"Where are we going today?" asked Jack.

"We will leave our horses at the end of the road," said Cowboy Hal. "Then we will walk up to timber line. That is a good place to see animals."

"What is timber line?" asked Jack.

"It is where the last trees are," said Cowboy Hal. "Above timber line there are no trees. Trees do not grow on the tops of high mountains."

Jack looked at the mountains as he rode along. He could see that the tops were bare. "Where do animals hide if there are no trees?" he asked.

"Wait and you will see," said Cowboy Hal.

There was a stream at the end of the road. Here they left their horses in a place where there was grass. They left the horses near enough to the water so they could drink.

Then Jack and Cowboy Hal began to climb. Up and up the trail they went. The trail was through the woods at first. Then they came to a place where only a few trees grew in the cracks of the rocks. The trees looked as if they were having a hard time to grow.

"Are we near the timber line now?" asked Jack.

"Yes," replied Cowboy Hal. "We'll soon be there."

All at once the trees were behind them. They were above timber line.

"Oh! Look ahead!" cried Jack. "Look at all the big rocks!"

"We'll soon be walking around those big rocks," said Cowboy Hal.

When they got to the rocks they had to go more slowly. They sat down to rest. "I'm glad I ate a big breakfast. I bet I couldn't have climbed up here if I hadn't," said Jack. "Oh! look on that rock! What is it?"

"Let's get a little closer," said Cowboy Hal. "Walk quietly so we won't scare it."

"I never saw an animal like that," said Jack. "Could we take it back with us? Will it bite?"

"No, we can't take it back," said Cowboy Hal. "And we won't get close enough to it to let it bite us."

"It's sitting up! It looks something like a squirrel. But it's bigger! Is it eating?" said Jack all in one breath.

"Yes, it is eating," said Cowboy Hal. "Can you see what it is?"

They hid behind a rock and peeped over the top. Still they could not see very well.

"Let's go to that rock over there. It is closer to the animal," said Jack.

Slowly they crept along. The animal stopped eating. It looked all around.

"Sh-h-h-h," said Cowboy Hal. "Keep very still. Don't say a word."

They could see very well now. "It's eating a green twig," whispered Jack.

Cowboy Hal looked at the animal. It was sitting on its hind legs and holding the green twig in its paws.

"I know what it is," he whispered. "It's a—watch out, Jack!" Jack had fallen down. "Did you hurt yourself?"

"No," answered Jack. "But I bet I scared the animal."

They looked up. The animal was gone!

"Too bad!" said Cowboy Hal. "That was a woodchuck."

"A woodchuck!" cried Jack. "We have woodchucks down on the prairie, but they don't look like this one!"

"Woodchucks live all over the country," said Cowboy Hal. "Woodchucks that live above timber line do not look just like those that live on the prairie."

Back at timber line Jack found a hole. "Is it a woodchuck's hole?" he asked.

"Yes," replied Cowboy Hal. "Woodchucks live in holes like that. They stay in the holes at night. Sometimes they run into their holes during the day if they hear or see an enemy."

"Do woodchucks stay in their holes all winter?" asked Jack.

"Yes," said Cowboy Hal. "They hibernate."

The Woodchuck

Two weeks later Jack and Cowboy Hal went back to timber line. They looked all around. There were no woodchucks.

"I guess they are hibernating," said Jack.

As Jack and Cowboy Hal started down the mountain they came to some men who were digging.

"We are making a trail," one of the men told Cowboy Hal. "Then people can ride horses up here if they wish."

As Jack and Cowboy Hal were watching the men, one of them called to Jack.

"Hi, boy! Come over here and see what I've found."

"Stick your hand into this hole," said the man. Jack stuck his hand into the hole. "I don't feel anything," he said.

"Reach way in," said the man.

"Whee!" cried Jack jumping back. "I felt something. It was soft and warm and furry. Cowboy Hal, you feel."

Cowboy Hal reached into the hole. Then he smiled. "Let's dig away a little of the dirt so we can look in."

Jack dug away some dirt with his hands. He looked into the hole. "Oh, Cowboy Hal, look here. What is it? What is it? I never saw anything like it."

Cowboy Hal stooped down. He put his two hands into the hole and lifted out an animal.

"Why, that's a woodchuck, isn't it?" cried Jack. "It is hibernating! My! How fat it is."

"Yes, woodchucks eat a great deal of food before hibernating," said Cowboy Hal.

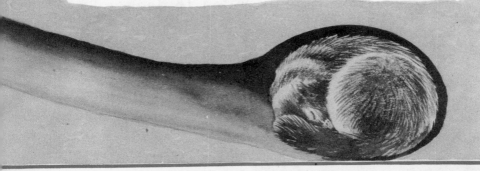

"Won't this fellow wake up?" asked Jack.

"We'll see," said Cowboy Hal. He put the woodchuck on a rock in the sun. Soon the woodchuck began to move. It looked around. Then it slid off the rock and slowly went away.

"It will crawl into another hole," said Cowboy Hal. "All woodchucks are hibernating now."

Cowboy Hal and Jack started down the trail. Jack stopped to rest. "I am tired," he said. "I'm hungry, too."

"We'll soon be home and have dinner," said Cowboy Hal. "We have used up a lot of food this morning. Now we need to eat more food."

Suddenly Jack whispered, "I hear something."

"I hear something too," said Cowboy Hal. "I wonder what it is."

"It's over that way," said Jack, pointing to the right.

"Let's crawl on top of this big rock and look around," said Cowboy Hal.

They climbed to the top of the rock. "Look over there!" whispered Jack. "Look! It's going up the mountain! It's a bear!" Jack was all out of breath.

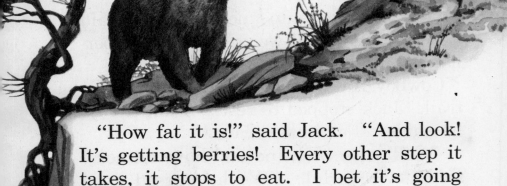

"How fat it is!" said Jack. "And look! It's getting berries! Every other step it takes, it stops to eat. I bet it's going to hibernate."

"Maybe it is," Cowboy Hal said. "Bears do hibernate."

"Do bears always eat a lot before they hibernate?" asked Jack.

"Yes, they do," said Cowboy Hal. "They have to be fat enough to live all winter without eating."

They watched the bear disappear into the woods.

Jack Learns About His Bones

Cowboy Hal and Jack took many long rides. Sometimes they were gone all day. Sometimes they got lost. Cowboy Hal carried a compass. The compass was a great help when they were lost. Cowboy Hal and Jack would look at the compass. Then they knew which way to go. The compass needle always pointed north. This is a compass.

Sometimes Cowboy Hal let Jack carry the compass. Then Jack would watch the compass and call out to Cowboy Hal, "Now we are on the right trail. I know because we are south of the ranch. The compass tells me we are going north."

When Cowboy Hal and Jack were gone all day, they always stopped for dinner. They built a camp fire and cooked their dinner over it. They let their horses eat grass. Sometimes Cowboy Hal and Jack would catch fish and cook them. Jack liked to catch fish. He liked to eat them, too.

One day Cowboy Hal and Jack caught some fish. They cooked the fish until they were nice and brown. Jack was hungry. He was eating a fish. He got some bones in his mouth.

"I wish fish didn't have any bones," said Jack. "Bones get in my mouth."

"Bones *are* a lot of trouble when you eat fish," said Cowboy Hal. "But fish would be funny animals without bones. They wouldn't have any shape. Cattle, horses, sheep, and many other animals must have bones. You and I must have bones. Bones are very useful."

"I guess that's right," said Jack. "If Rat Tail didn't have bones, I couldn't ride him."

"If you didn't have bones," said Cowboy Hal, "you couldn't walk. In fact, you couldn't do anything You couldn't run, ride, sit up, or stand up without bones. Bones give you your shape, too."

"Do bones grow?" asked Jack. "Do they grow bigger when I get bigger?"

"Yes," said Cowboy Hal. "Your bones grow. You should always remember to feed your bones."

"How can I feed my bones?" asked Jack.

"By eating foods that make bones grow," said Cowboy Hal. "Milk, eggs, lettuce, beans, and spinach are all good bone food."

"You should always remember to sit up straight and stand up straight," Cowboy Hal added. "Sitting and standing straight help your bones grow straight."

The Doctor Comes

Jimmy was not in school. The children missed him. He was the leader of the band. The band was to play for the children's mothers that afternoon.

"Maybe Jimmy is sick," said Nancy. "I saw the doctor go to his house."

The children were sorry that a doctor had gone to Jimmy's house. They were sorry that Jimmy was sick. Miss Parker said they might choose another leader for the band. So the children chose Jane. Jane was sorry Jimmy could not be there, but Jane led the band. The children said she did it very well. Miss Parker said that Jane was a good leader.

Jimmy's mother did not come to hear the band.

"Maybe Jimmy's mother is sick, too," said Nancy. "We had better go and see. Maybe we can see Jimmy, too."

The children chose Bob to go to Jimmy's house. Bob soon came running back. He was all out of breath.

"A man was putting a sign on Jimmy's house," Bob said. "The sign says that no one can go in or out of the house."

"Why was he putting the sign on Jimmy's house?" asked Nancy.

"I know," said Bob. "I went home and asked Mother. She said he was putting up the sign because Jimmy has scarlet fever. The sign keeps other boys and girls away. We might catch scarlet fever from Jimmy. We must keep away from Jimmy's house until he is well."

"Jimmy is in *quarantine*," said Miss Parker.

"Quarantine is a new word," said Nancy. Miss Parker wrote it on the blackboard. The children liked the new word. They learned it.

"Quarantine signs help us keep well," said Bob. "They tell us to keep away from children who are sick."

Jimmy did not come back to school for a long time. The children did not visit him. The quarantine sign stayed on the house.

Jimmy was in bed. He was very sick. He didn't want to play. Each day the children wrote him a letter. Jimmy liked the letters. Sometimes he saw the children as they went home from school.

Jimmy stayed in bed until he was well. Then a man took down the quarantine sign. Jimmy went back to school. He was happy to be with the children again. He told them all about scarlet fever. He brought the quarantine sign to school to show the children.

"I had a sign on my house when I had scarlet fever," said Dick. "It kept the other children away. But I did not know our new word then. I did not know I was in quarantine."

"I saw a quarantine sign on another house today," said Bob. "I saw a doctor come out of the house. I asked him what the sign was for. He said diphtheria."

"My brother had diphtheria," said Jane. "He was very, very sick."

"Did you have a sign on your house?" asked Susan.

"Yes, we had a sign on the house for a long time," said Jane. "No one could come to our house. The doctor wouldn't let me go away from the house either."

"Did you get diphtheria, too?" asked Nancy.

"No, the nurse wouldn't let any of us go into my brother's room. We didn't get diphtheria. When my brother was well, a man came and took down the sign. Then I could play with my brother. We went to school and no one else got diphtheria."

"The nurse sent me home from school because I had a cold," said Bob. "I had to stay home for three days. The doctor came to see me. But there was no sign on our house. Can't you give a cold to another child?"

"Yes, you can give a cold to another child," said Miss Parker. "But you aren't quarantined when you have a cold."

"Why aren't you quarantined when you have a cold?" asked Jimmy.

"Let's ask the nurse," said Miss Parker. The nurse told the children about quarantine signs. "Quarantine signs are used to keep children away from disease. If you visit a child who has scarlet fever or diphtheria, you may get sick. A quarantine sign is not put up for every disease. But the sick children have to stay home. Other children should not visit them. A quarantine sign is not put up for a cold. But the doctor tells you to keep away from children who have colds. Be very careful when you have a cold. Then you will not give it to another child."

Reading Thermometers

"I looked at the outside thermometer this morning," said Bob. "The red line was down to 40. That means the days are getting colder. We have to wear warm clothes now."

"What makes the red line in the thermometer go up and down?" asked Susan.

"The temperature of the air makes the red line go up and down," said Miss Parker. "The thermometer shows the temperature of the air. If the air is cold, the red line is short. It is short today. It is at 40."

"The thermometer in the schoolroom says it is 70," said Nancy.

"The air in the schoolroom is warmer than the air out of doors," said Jimmy. "When the air is warmer, the red line in the thermometer is longer. I remember a day last summer. The thermometer was at 90. The air was very hot that day."

Which thermometer shows a cold day?
Which thermometer shows a hot day?

Another Thermometer

Nancy did not feel well. Miss Parker said, "Nancy, you had better go to the school nurse."

The nurse said, "I must take your temperature." She put a thermometer into Nancy's mouth. Nancy kept her mouth closed for two minutes. Then the nurse looked at the thermometer.

"You do not have a fever," said the nurse. "Your temperature is just right."

Nancy was glad that she did not have a fever. She asked. "May I look at that thermometer? It doesn't look like the thermometer we have in our school room."

"Your school room thermometer is on a board. It is made to hang on the wall," said the nurse.

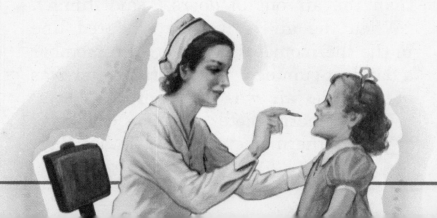

Nancy looked at the nurse's thermometer. "It has numbers," she said. "Our school thermometer has numbers, too."

"Yes, this thermometer is very much like the one in Miss Parker's room," said the nurse. "But this one is made to put into your mouth."

"Our school thermometer tells us how hot our room is," said Nancy. "Does this one tell how hot my mouth is?"

"Yes, and it tells how hot your body is," said the nurse. "Your temperature is a little above 98 when you are well."

"Was Jimmy's temperature more than 98 when he was sick?" asked Nancy.

"Yes," said the nurse. "Jimmy had a fever when he had scarlet fever."

Nancy went back to her room. She told the children about the thermometer.

"The nurse put the thermometer into my mouth. I kept my mouth closed tight. The thermometer told how hot my body was. My temperature is about 98 and I do not have a fever. My temperature would be higher than 98 if I had a fever."

Experiments

The children gathered around a table. Miss Parker had something new for them.

There were two bottles on the table. Each bottle had a cork in it. In each cork was a small funnel.

"Goody!" said Susan. "This is an experiment. What do you suppose we will do?"

The children turned to Miss Parker.

"Can you pour some water into the bottles?" she asked.

"*I* can," said Jimmy, thinking it would be easy. He poured some water into the funnel of one bottle. The funnel filled quickly. Water ran down on the table.

"That's funny," said Jimmy. He looked closely at the bottle. "Ho! This bottle is filled already. It has water in it. That's why I couldn't pour any more water into this bottle!"

Jimmy took the cork out of the other bottle. He looked at the bottle closely. He turned it upside down. He smiled. "This one is empty. I'll fill it." He put the cork and funnel back into the bottle. He poured some water into the funnel. The water ran out on the table!

The children laughed.

"That's funny," said Jimmy. "The bottle is empty. Why doesn't the water run into it?"

"There must be something in the bottle we can't see," said Jane.

The children looked again. No one could see a thing in the bottle.

Miss Parker smiled. "Eyes can't see it, hands can't feel it, round about us everywhere," she said.

"Oh, that's air," said Jimmy. "But air wouldn't keep the water from running into the bottle."

"Oh, yes, it would," said Miss Parker. "The air in the bottle must get out before anything else can get in."

Jimmy tipped the bottle a little. He tried pouring in some water very slowly. The water ran in. Tipping the bottle let the water push the air out.

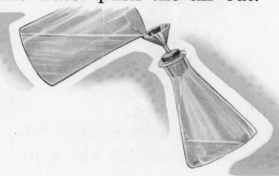

"Air is everywhere," said Susan. "There is air in this room."

"But we can't see the air," said Nancy. "We can't taste it."

"We can't smell it," said Bob. "Air is really something and yet we can't see or taste or smell it!"

"Do you want to try another experiment?" asked Miss Parker.

"Oh, yes," the children said.

This is the experiment Miss Parker let the children try:

1. Fill a dish with water.
2. Put a cork on top of the water.

3. Put a glass over the cork and push the glass to the bottom of the dish.
4. See what happens.

"What made the cork go to the bottom of the dish?" asked Jimmy.

"That glass was full of air. You pushed the glass down in the water. The air couldn't get out. The air pushed the water away. Then the cork went to the bottom of the dish," said Miss Parker.

Miss Parker had something else for the children to do. It was time for them to drink their milk. Miss Parker had put a straw through a hole in each milk bottle cap.

"That's funny," said Dick when he tried to drink. "I can't get the milk to come out of here, Miss Parker."

"I can't," said Susan.

"I can't," said Bob.

"Take the caps from the bottles," said Miss Parker. "Now try it."

Now the children could get the milk.

"Why couldn't we drink our milk when the caps were on the bottles?" asked Bob.

"The caps kept out the air. When you suck on a straw, you do not suck up the milk. You suck the air out of the straw. The straw is empty. The air presses down on the milk and makes it come up into the empty straw," Miss Parker told them.

"Oh, I see," said Susan. "We had to take off the caps so the air could get to the milk."

"Can anyone turn a glass of water upside down without spilling it?" asked Miss Parker.

"I can," said Bob. He filled a glass with water. He put a piece of paper over the top of the glass. He turned it upside down. The water did not run out.

"What keeps the water from running out?" asked Jane.

"The paper keeps it from running out," said Jimmy.

"Let's try it again," said Miss Parker. "But let's put a piece of cheesecloth over the glass."

This time Susan turned the glass upside down. The water stayed in the glass.

"I don't understand what keeps the water from running out," said Jane.

"It must be the air," said Jimmy. "We just learned that the air presses down on things. Does the air press up on things, too, Miss Parker? Does the air keep the water from running out of the glass?"

"Yes, it does, Jimmy. The air presses up on this paper and cloth and keeps the water from running out," said Miss Parker.

"Air presses up and down," said Susan.

"Air can do work for us, too," said Miss Parker.

"I'll show you a way air works for us," said Jimmy.

This was Jimmy's experiment:

1. He put a paper bag under a book.
2. He blew into the bag.
3. The paper bag slowly filled with air. As it filled, it raised the book.

The children liked Jimmy's experiment.

"We can raise things with air," said Bob. "Air works for us."

"Now I'll show you another way that air works," said Miss Parker. She held up a medicine dropper. All the children had seen a medicine dropper before.

"This is an air machine," said Miss Parker. "A machine does work. Here is some flour." She pressed on the rubber end of the dropper and put it near the flour. Then she let go of the rubber end. Some flour went up into the glass.

Bob tried it and the same thing happened. "When I pressed on the rubber end, I pressed the air out of the tube. When I let go of the rubber end, the outside air pressed the flour into the tube."

"Now you know that air presses up and down. You also know that air works for you," said Miss Parker.

The children did some other experiments with air. They learned that air helps us in many ways. They learned that air helps in these machines.

Why Susan's Balloon Burst

One day Susan brought a balloon to school. It was a bright red balloon. Susan showed it to the children and then she hung it on the radiator. Susan forgot about her balloon until she heard a noise. Pop!

"Oh, my balloon!" cried Susan. "It burst! Oh, dear! Why did it burst?"

Miss Parker said, "We will do an experiment and then you will find out why it burst."

Miss Parker had a thin glass bottle. She put a cork in the bottle. In the cork was a bent glass tube. It looked like this.

"I will put the bottle outside the window and let it get very cold," said Miss Parker. "Then we can do our experiment."

When the bottle was cold, Miss Parker brought it into the room again. She set the cold bottle on the table and put the tube in a pan of water.

"Who has warm hands?" she asked.

"I have," said Nancy.

"That's fine," said Miss Parker. "Nancy, will you please put your hands around the cold bottle?"

Nancy put her hands around the bottle. In a few minutes bubbles came into the water.

"What makes the bubbles in the water?" asked Jimmy. "There isn't anything in the bottle."

"Oh, yes, there is, Jimmy," Jane told him. "Don't you remember the bottle in the other experiment?"

"Now I remember," said Jimmy. "It had air in it."

"There is air in this bottle, too," said Miss Parker.

"Those must be air bubbles that come into the water," said Susan.

"What makes them come out of the bottle?" asked Dick.

"Maybe the air swelled," said Jimmy. "Maybe it got too big for the bottle."

"It did," said Miss Parker. "Do you know what made it get too big?"

The children thought for a while.

"The bottle was very cold," said Nancy. "I put my hands on it. My hands warmed the bottle."

"Maybe the warm bottle warmed the air inside it," said Jimmy. "Did the air swell because it got warm?"

"Air takes up more room when it gets warmer," said Miss Parker. "But we do not say that air swells. We say that air *expands* when it gets warmer."

"I guess the air in my balloon expanded," said Susan. "The radiator made the air expand and expand until the rubber stretched as much as it could. Then the air just burst through the rubber!"

The children laughed. Now Susan did not feel so bad about her balloon.

"Last summer we were out in our car on a hot day. We had a blow-out," said Bob. "The air in the tire expanded. The air took up so much room it didn't have any place to go. It just blew up the tire. It made a big noise, too."

While the children were learning that air expands when it is warmed, the bottle had grown cold.

"Oh, look!" cried Jimmy. "Some of the water has gone up into the tube!"

"When air cools, it takes up less room," said Miss Parker. "The air in the bottle cooled while we were talking. There was some room left in the tube. The outside air pressed on the water in the pan. The air pushed the water into the tube."

"What do you call that?" asked Jane.

"We say air *contracts* when it gets cooler," said Miss Parker. "Cool air takes up less room than warm air."

"The air in the bottle expanded when my warm hands were on the bottle," said Nancy. "It contracted when I took my warm hands away."

What Makes Sound?

Christmas is the time for toys—toys for little children and for big children. Little children like toys that make noise. They like drums and horns and rattles.

Jimmy and Dick were too big to play with horns and rattles, but they wanted to find out what made the noise. They decided to do some experiments at home.

Jimmy did an experiment with a rattle. He took it apart. It was made of tin. It had some hard balls inside. Jimmy put it together. He took it by the handle. When he shook the rattle, the balls struck against the tin. That made the noise.

Then Jimmy held the rattle by the tin ball. It didn't make much noise.

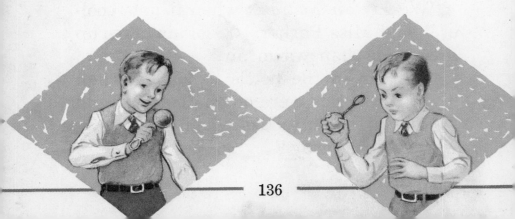

Jimmy's father said, "Take it by the handle. Shake it. Now put your finger on the tin ball. Can you feel anything?"

"I can feel it move," he said. "It moves back and forth. It moves fast."

"When things move like that, we say they *vibrate*," said Jimmy's father.

"When I hold the rattle by the tin part, it can't vibrate very much," said Jimmy. "It doesn't make much noise."

Dick did an experiment with a drum. He beat it with sticks. It made a loud noise. He put his hand on the head of the drum. "It vibrates, too," he said.

"Yes, it does," said Jimmy's father. "Let Jimmy put his hand on the drum head. Now you beat it."

The drum did not make much noise.

"Must a thing vibrate to make sound?" asked Jimmy.

"Yes," said his father. "If you hold the drum head so it can not vibrate at all, it will make no sound."

"Let's experiment with this horn," said Jimmy. He blew the horn. It made a very loud noise. Then he held it tight in his hand and blew. The sound was still loud.

"The horn doesn't vibrate when I blow it," he said. "Where does the sound come from?"

"It comes from the inside," said Dick. "Let's take it apart."

The boys opened the horn. Inside they found something that looked like this.

Jimmy's father said it was a reed.

Jimmy blew the horn. The reed vibrated. He put his finger on the reed. He blew. But the horn made no sound.

Next day the boys told the children about sound. Jimmy showed them the rattle. He showed them how it made sounds. He let the children feel the rattle vibrate.

Dick told the children about the drum. He let them beat it. They felt the drum head vibrate.

Both boys showed the children the horn. They opened it so the children could see the reed. They blew the horn. The children could see the reed vibrate.

The children experimented with a bell. It made a sound when it was struck. They felt the bell vibrate. It did not make much sound when Jane put her hand on the bell. The bell could not vibrate much.

"A thing must vibrate to make sound," said Jimmy. "I must remember that."

The Winter Lunch Counter

The children had a feeding shelf for birds. They called it a lunch counter for birds.

"I'm going to keep a record of all the birds I see at the lunch counter," said Susan.

Susan wrote all these names in one week:

Nuthatch

Chickadee

Junco

Sparrow

Horned lark

Cardinal

Blue jay

Goldfinch

Downy woodpecker

Here are pictures of these birds. Can you match the pictures and the names?

Susan wrote about the birds that came to the lunch counter. Each time she wrote about different birds.

Wednesday: I saw a little gray bird at the lunch counter today. It was a goldfinch. The last time I saw it, it was yellow and black. Now it is gray and black. It has molted. *Molted* means that it has lost its old feathers. As it lost its old feathers, new ones grew. Its old feathers were yellow. Its new feathers are not yellow. They are gray. Its wing feathers are still black.

Friday: The cardinal is not as bright as it was in the summer. It did not molt in autumn. It did not lose its feathers, but the ends of its feathers wore off. I still think it is the prettiest bird that comes to the lunch counter.

Monday: The blue jay doesn't look as blue as it did. It did not molt in autumn. It did not lose its feathers. Its feathers wore off, too. The blue jay doesn't go south in the winter. I'm glad it stays here. I like blue jays.

Tuesday: The horned lark will not eat at the lunch counter. It eats on the ground. The sparrows ate on the ground with the horned lark. There were no new birds at the lunch counter today.

Wednesday: Chickadees and nuthatches were here today. Chickadees live here all the year round. I like to watch them get their food. I like to watch a nuthatch go down a tree head first.

The juncoes are here. They migrate from the north. They are here only in winter. In summer they go back north. Sometimes they are called snow birds.

Thursday: Today a downy woodpecker was eating at our lunch counter. It was eating suet. Some birds do not eat suet. Seed-eaters like sparrows do not eat suet. But insect-eaters like the downy woodpecker eat suet.

On our lunch counter we have different kinds of food. We have seeds for the seed-eaters and suet for the insect-eaters. Some of the birds eat nuts and bread, too. Cardinals will eat apples.

A Ground Bird

"There are tracks in the snow," said Susan one day as she came into school. "They look like tracks of small chickens." The children went outside to see them.

"Those are quail tracks," said Miss Parker. "The quail are looking for food. The snow has covered up all their food."

"We'll have to put out some food for them," said Nancy. "What do quail eat?"

"Quail are something like chickens," said Dick. "Maybe they eat the things chickens eat."

"Yes, they do," said Miss Parker. "They will eat cracked corn or oats."

Miss Parker showed the children how to make a shelter for the quail. They made a tent of corn stalks. They put some corn and oats in the tent. The quail soon found the food. They ate all of it.

Quail are something like chickens but they are much smaller. They have heavy bodies. They have short rounded wings. They can not fly very far and they do not migrate. When snow covers their food, they come into towns and farms looking for something to eat.

The children saw quail tracks nearly every day. They saw other tracks, too. They often saw dog tracks. Sometimes they saw rabbit tracks and squirrel tracks. Can you tell which animals made these tracks?

Beaks and Feet

"What is that noise?" asked Dick's father as he opened the garage door. Something was flying against the window.

"It's a bird," Dick cried.

It was a little brown and white bird that had found a warm place to sleep away from the snow storm. Dick caught the bird and took it into the house.

"It is a brown creeper," said Dick's mother when she saw it. "Brown creepers come down from the north to spend the winter."

Mother took the little brown and white bird in her hand. It shivered, then lay still. But its eyes showed that it was very much alive.

Dick had never seen a bird just like it. Its beak was slender and curved.

Mother said, "The brown creeper uses its beak to get insects from the cracks in the tree bark. The color of the brown creeper is so much like the tree that it can hide easily."

When the little bird was warm, Dick and Mother took it outside and put it on the trunk of a tree. It went around and around the tree looking for insects.

"You won't find any insects this cold day," said Dick. "You'd better go to our feeding shelf. It has suet for you."

The queerest thing about the brown creeper was its tail. The feathers were stiff and pointed, very much like the tail feathers of the downy woodpecker. Its tail helped the bird hold itself against the tree when it was getting insects.

The creeper's claws were sharp. It could hold on easily to the bark.

A brown creeper starts eating at the bottom of a tree. It goes around and around the tree, always going higher as it goes around. Soon it gets to the top of the tree. Then it flies down to the bottom and begins all over again.

If you look at birds carefully, you will see that their beaks and feet help them get their food.

Many insects hide in the cracks of the bark of trees. Some birds eat these insects. The brown creeper eats them. The brown creeper's beak is too slender for it to dig a hole in the bark.

Nuthatches have stronger beaks than creepers. Their beaks are straight. They can go deeper into the bark than creepers can.

Woodpeckers have the strongest beaks of all. They can dig holes right through the bark with their beaks. Then they use their pointed tongues to catch the insects that are hidden there.

Orioles eat insects, too, but they do not get them from the bark of trees. A mother oriole feeds her babies caterpillars. Sometimes she feeds them small grasshoppers and small moths. The beaks of orioles are long and pointed. They are just the kind to catch and hold a wiggling caterpillar.

The robin has a long, pointed beak, too. Its beak helps it get earthworms. Its beak helps it get berries, too.

Birds like the robin can eat many kinds of food. But some birds can eat only one kind of food because of the shape of their beaks. The brown creeper eats insects. It can not get worms from the ground.

A cardinal has a short, thick beak. It can crack big sunflower seeds easily. Its beak is very strong and heavy. It can not get insects from the bark of trees. Its beak is too short and thick.

The beak of a goldfinch is not as large as the beak of a cardinal. But goldfinches also have seed eating beaks. Goldfinches can often be seen sitting on the stems of wild plants. They are picking the seeds out of the plants.

A swallow's beak opens wide. A swallow flies through the air with its mouth wide open. It sweeps up the mosquitoes and other insects that are in its path. Swallows do not get insects from trees as brown creepers or woodpeckers do.

The feet of birds often help them. Birds have no hands so they use their feet and beaks to build nests. Robins carry mud in their beaks and fasten their nests together with it. They use their feet to help shape the mud.

Chickens and quail use their feet to help them get food. They scratch in the grass and dirt to find insects. Their feet and legs are strong. They have sharp claws.

Ducks have webs between their toes. Their feet help them swim. They can't scratch in the dirt the way chickens do.

The feet of many birds help them sit on a branch or wire. Did you ever wonder why a sparrow doesn't fall off a branch when it goes to sleep? Its toes go around the branch and hold it tight.

Birds that spend most of their time flying have very weak feet. Swallows have weak feet.

Can you tell how these feet are used?

How to Make Feeding Shelves

Joyce was always doing something new. This time she wanted to make a feeding shelf for the birds.

Uncle Don and Ted laughed at her but Joyce did not mind. "You must wait and see. I'll have birds eating at the window before you know it," said Joyce.

There are not many birds in a big city. Birds do not often fly near tall apartment houses. But that did not keep Joyce from making a feeding shelf.

She read in books about feeding shelves for birds and how to make them. She learned that a very simple feeding shelf is the best kind to make. She fastened a board outside the window. On it she put some pieces of suet, some cracked nuts, and some seeds.

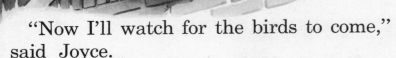

"Now I'll watch for the birds to come," said Joyce.

Joyce watched for a long time. But not a bird came. How disappointed Joyce was! "I wonder where all the birds can be," she said. "I've waited and waited and not one has come to my feeding shelf."

Uncle Don told her what she should do.

"Birds won't know what this shelf is. You should make the birds think it is part of the woods. Get some evergreen branches and put them on the shelf. The branches will make the shelf look like a tree. The branches will also cover the shelf from the storms and make a dry place where the birds may eat."

Joyce got some evergreen branches. She got them from an old Christmas tree. She put the branches on the shelf. She tied some suet to the branches. She put some more seeds on the shelf.

Again she watched and watched. And this time one English sparrow found the shelf. It sat on the shelf and ate. It was hungry. It had found a cozy eating place away from the storm. There are not many places like this in a big city.

The next day three English sparrows ate at the feeding shelf.

"The birds must have seen the other sparrow eat here," said Joyce. "Then they came, too."

"Yes," said Uncle Don. "Birds are like that. They watch each other. If they see a bird getting food from a tree, they go there, too. Maybe these birds saw the first sparrow eating here. They came along to eat."

Soon there were many sparrows eating at the feeding shelf.

"I want other birds to eat at the feeding shelf," said Joyce. "The English sparrows eat up all the food. There is none left for other birds."

"We'll fix the feeding shelf," said Uncle Don. "English sparrows are afraid of a shelf that swings. We'll fix this shelf so that it will swing. Maybe the sparrows will stop coming."

Uncle Don helped Joyce fix the shelf. He fixed the shelf so that it would swing. The sparrows would not eat there. But the juncoes would. They came to the feeding shelf and ate the seeds that Joyce put out for them.

Joyce put out some suet. Some chickadees came and ate it. Joyce laughed, "See! I have a good feeding shelf."

Feeding Shelves

There are many kinds of feeding shelves. You can make one very easily. Here are some pictures of feeding shelves.

This is a very easy feeding shelf to make. Nail a narrow board to the window sill. The board will keep the seeds and suet from rolling off the sill. You can do this easily.

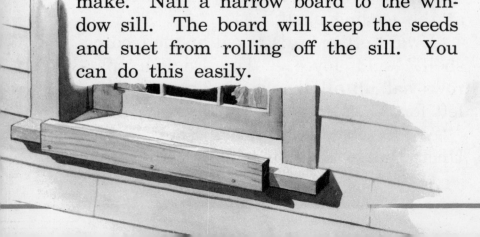

This feeding shelf is made from the bottom of a barrel. It has evergreen branches around it to make it look like the woods. Part of the barrel is used over the top of the shelf. Can you fix a feeding shelf like this one?

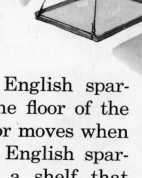

This is a feeding shelf that English sparrows do not like. It is made like a swing.

This is a feeding box. English sparrows will not eat at it. The floor of the box is on a spring. The floor moves when the sparrows stand on it. English sparrows do not often eat at a shelf that moves.

Day and Night

"What makes day and night?" asked Nancy one day.

"We will do an experiment and see if we can find out," said Miss Parker. "Bob may be the earth. His nose may be the town in which we live." The children laughed and looked at Bob's nose.

"Let's use the desk light for the sun," said Dick. "It shines like the sun."

"The earth turns around, so Bob must turn around," said Miss Parker.

"How shall I turn?" asked Bob.

"Turn around slowly," said Miss Parker.

Bob turned so that the desk light shone on his nose. "Now it is day in our town," he said. Bob kept on turning.

"The sun isn't shining in our town now," said Jane as Bob turned away from the light. "It must be night!"

Bob kept on turning and then the light shone on his nose again. The children cried, "Now it's day again!"

Bob stopped and asked, "How long does it take the earth to turn all the way around?"

"Twenty-four hours," said Jimmy.

"Twenty-four hours!" said Nancy "That's a whole day and night!"

"If the earth turns around every twenty-four hours, the sun can't shine on our town all the time," said Jane. "Sometimes our town is turned away from the sun. Sometimes it is turned toward the sun."

"That is why we have day and night," said Nancy. "Other boys and girls are having night right now. They live on the other side of the earth."

"That is right," said Miss Parker. "It is always night some place. It is day some place. When we have night here, it is day on the other side of the earth."

The children wanted to do the experiment again.

When the light shone on Bob's nose, the children said, "It's noon."

When the light shone on Bob's right ear, they said, "It's sunset."

When the light shone on the back of Bob's head, they said, "It's midnight."

When the sun shone on his left ear, they said, "It's sunrise."

"Now I see that the sun shines on our town only part of the time," said Nancy. "Now I see why we have night and day."

Miss Parker let them do another experiment. This time they used the desk light and a large ball. She said, "The earth is like a ball, you know."

"That ball will turn around," said Jimmy. "It spins almost like a top."

"Yes, and the earth spins around much as a top does," said Miss Parker. "How long does it take the earth to turn all the way around?"

"Twenty-four hours," answered Bob.

Miss Parker smiled. "I guess you will always remember that, won't you, Bob? Now, Jimmy, you may turn the ball. And Susan, you may put a mark on the place where our town is."

Miss Parker wrote on the blackboard:

1. Jimmy may turn the ball so that Pleasant Valley is having night.

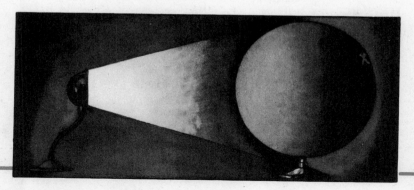

2. Jimmy may turn the ball so that
Pleasant Valley is having day.

3. Jimmy may turn the ball so that
Pleasant Valley is having sunset.

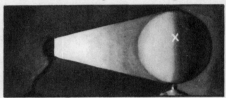

When Jimmy had done these things,
he said, "This experiment shows us that
the earth turns around and that is why
we have night and day. The sun cannot
shine on all parts of the earth at the
same time."

"What is the earth?" asked Jane.

"The earth is a heavenly body," said
Miss Parker.

"A star is a heavenly body," said Jane.
"Is the earth a star?"

"No, the earth is not a star," said Miss
Parker. "Stars are hot. The earth is
not hot. Stars shine. The earth does
not shine. The sun is a star. It shines.
We get heat and light from the sun."

The Moon

"Miss Parker, did you see the full moon last night?" asked Jimmy the next morning.

"Yes, I did," she answered. "It was so bright and large that I could not help seeing it."

"What makes it shine?" asked Nancy.

"Well, it just shines," said Bob.

"That is not a very good answer," said Miss Parker. "Would you really like to know what makes the moon shine?"

"Oh, yes," cried the children.

"The moon is round like the earth," said Miss Parker. "But it has no light of its own. We can not see the moon unless the sun shines on it. The sun shines on the moon just as it shines on the earth. At night we can see the moon because the sun is shining on it. The moon can be seen only when the sun shines on it. Let's do an experiment."

The children always liked experiments.

They made the room dark. Miss Parker gave Susan something to hold. "Can you see what is in Susan's hand?" she asked.

"No," cried the children. "It's dark."

Miss Parker turned on the desk light. "Susan has a ball in her hand," said Bob. "We can see it when the light is on."

"Let's play that the ball is the moon," said Miss Parker. "The desk light will be the sun. Now let's make the room dark again."

"We can't see the moon when the sun isn't shining on it," cried Jane.

Miss Parker turned on the desk light.

"Now we can see the moon," said Susan. "We can see the moon when the sun shines on it."

"Yes, that's right," said Miss Parker. "The moon does not have light of its own. The light we see is the sun's light shining on it. We see the moon because the sun shines on it."

"But why does the moon have different shapes?" asked Dick.

"The moon moves around the earth," said Miss Parker. "We'll do another experiment. We'll let Nancy be the earth. Bob may be the moon. The moon moves around the earth. Bob, you walk slowly around Nancy. Keep your face toward her all the time. Nancy, you keep your face toward Bob. The desk light will be the sun. Let's have it shine on Bob's face."

"All of Bob's face is in the light," said Nancy.

"That's like a full moon," said Jane.

Bob kept on moving.

"Now I can see only part of Bob's face," said Nancy.

"Now Bob's face is dark," said Nancy.
"That is like the new moon," said Miss
Parker. "We can not see the new moon
the first night."

Bob moved just a little.
This is the way he looked
to Nancy. "I've seen the
moon look like that!" she
cried.

At last Bob had moved around so the
light shone full on his face again.

"That's the full moon again," shouted
the children.

"Yes," said Miss Parker. "As the moon
moves around the earth it seems to change
shape. We can see only the part of the
moon that the sun shines on. Here are
some things to remember about the moon."
She wrote them on the blackboard:

1. The moon is round like a ball.
2. The moon gets its light from the sun.
3. The moon moves around the earth.

Miss Parker told the children, "The moon always stays near the earth. The moon travels around and around the earth all of the time. The earth travels around and around the sun all the time.

"Away out there in space is the sun. The sun is a bright star. It shines on our earth and gives us light. It shines on the moon and gives it light. If we could live on the moon, we could see the earth shining just as we see the moon. The sun would shine on the earth just as it shines on the moon."

"Which is the biggest, the sun or the earth or the moon?" asked Jimmy.

"The sun, I think," said Susan.

"Yes, it is," said Miss Parker. "The earth is bigger than the moon. The sun is very much bigger than the earth."

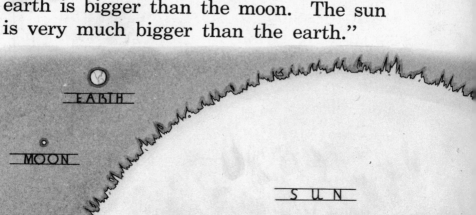

EARTH

MOON

SUN

Jimmy's Star Pictures

Jimmy found pictures of the north sky and the south sky in a book. He took them to school to show the children.

"Here is Orion in the south sky," he said. "And here is the Dog Star."

"I see the Big Dipper in the north sky," said Susan. "I see the Little Dipper, too."

"I see the North Star," said Bob.

"What's that picture?" asked Dick as he pointed to some stars in the north sky.

Jimmy said, "That picture is called Cassiopeia. Father told me a story about Cassiopeia last night.

"Cassiopeia was a very beautiful queen. She was a very proud queen. She boasted about her own beauty and her daughter's beauty. The gods did not like her because she boasted. The gods put Cassiopeia in a chair in the sky and she has been there ever since. Those stars are supposed to be her chair."

Jack's Clothing

"Bed time, Jack," called Mother.

"But, Mother, it's so cold I don't want to go to bed," said Jack. "It's below zero outside, and my room is cold."

"You may take off your clothes here by the stove," said Mother.

Jack got ready for bed. It was warm by the stove. But oh! how cold his bed was when he jumped into it! Mother tucked the covers all around him and said, "You will soon be warm."

After a few minutes Jack was warm. His bed was warm. "I must have a stove inside me," he laughed.

Mother laughed, too. "You don't have a stove inside you," she said, "but your body does make heat. When you cover yourself so that the heat can't get away, your bed gets warm."

In the morning Jack was still warm. His bed was still warm. But his room was cold. There was frost on the window.

Jack jumped out of bed and ran into the living room. He dressed by the big stove.

"Old stove," he said, "you can make heat to keep the house warm, but I can make heat, too. I kept my bed warm. I kept myself warm, too."

Cowboy Hal came in from the barn. He had been feeding the horses. He was cold.

"Is Rat Tail all right?" asked Jack. "Did he keep warm last night? Does he make heat as I do?"

"Yes, he does," said Cowboy Hal. "Rat Tail is all right. He makes heat. All of the animals on the ranch make heat. Rat Tail has a heavy coat of hair that helps keep the heat in him."

After breakfast Jack and Cowboy Hal went out to look at the animals. The sheep were busy eating. "Their wool keeps them warm," said Jack. "I wish I had a wool coat like that."

"You do have a coat made of wool," said Cowboy Hal. "You have it on right now. It is made of wool that came from a sheep. It keeps you warm, too."

"Are my stockings and mittens made of wool?" asked Jack. "They keep me warm."

"Yes, most of your winter clothes are made of wool. Wool keeps you warm just as wool keeps a sheep warm," said Cowboy Hal. "The sheep's body makes heat. The wool keeps the heat from getting away. That keeps the sheep warm."

When Jack went back to the house, he told his mother about the sheep.

"You have learned why you wear things made of wool in winter," said Mother. "Now tell me why you don't wear wool in the summer."

"I think I know," said Jack. "My body makes heat. If I wore clothes in summer that kept the heat in, I would be too warm. So in the summer I must wear clothes that let the heat out."

"That's right," said Mother. "And you should also know that clothes protect you. Shoes keep your feet from getting hurt. Mittens keep your hands warm. Your cap keeps your head and ears warm."

"If I had hair all over my body like Rat Tail, I wouldn't need clothes," said Jack. "Rat Tail's hair gets thick and warm in the winter. Then some of it comes out in the spring."

"You do have hairs all over your body," said Mother. "But you do not have enough hair to protect your body. Look at your arms. See the tiny hairs."

Jack looked at his arms. Sure enough, he could see hairs. But of course they were too tiny to keep his body warm.

"Wool keeps my body warm in winter," said Jack. "But children who live where it is warm in winter do not need to wear wool. I do not need wool in the summer."

"That is right," said Mother. "Some boys and girls live where the weather is always warm. They do not wear wool. They wear cotton clothing. You wear cotton clothing in the summer, too."

"What is cotton?" asked Jack. "What kind of animal does cotton come from?"

"It does not come from an animal," said Mother. "It comes from a plant. The plant grows where the summer is very long. Cotton is picked from the plant. Then it is made into cloth. It does not keep the heat in the body. Cotton is good to wear in hot weather. Silk is better to wear in hot weather than wool. But silk is not so good as cotton."

"Does silk come from an animal or a plant?" asked Jack.

"Silk does not grow on an animal. It does not grow on a plant. It comes from a cocoon," said Mother.

"A cocoon!" cried Jack. "Caterpillars make cocoons. Do caterpillars make silk?"

"Yes," said Mother. "Some caterpillars spin silk threads. They make cocoons. Then the silk of the cocoons is made into cloth. One kind of caterpillar that makes silk is called a silkworm."

"I must remember about clothing," said Jack. "Let me see. My body makes heat. In winter I wear clothing to keep the heat in. In summer I wear clothing that lets the heat out. Is that right?"

"Yes, it is," said Mother. "And you wear clothing to protect your body."

Silk is made by a caterpillar.　　Cotton comes from a plant.　　Wool comes from sheep.

Joyce's New Plant

Joyce liked the plants that were in the schoolroom. "I wish we had some plants at home," she said to her teacher.

"I'll give you a slip. Then you can raise your own plants," said the teacher.

"What is a slip?" asked Joyce.

"A slip is a cutting from a plant. I will cut a small branch from this geranium plant." The teacher cut the branch evenly with a sharp knife.

Then she gave it to Joyce. "See. I cut the branch so there is a bud on it. Take it home and put the cut end in water. Watch it and see what happens."

Joyce was very happy. She took the slip home. "See what I have," she cried to her mother. "It's a geranium slip. It will grow into a geranium plant."

"That's fine," said her mother. "I do hope it grows. Plants with flowers make a home pretty."

Joyce put the cut end of the slip into a glass of water. The next morning she looked at it. "It didn't do a thing!" she cried. "I thought it would grow!"

"Give it time," said Uncle Don. "Plants can't grow over night. Sometimes it takes several days. Sometimes it takes several weeks. You keep on watching. Something will happen."

Joyce looked at the plant every day. One morning she cried, "Ted! Uncle Don! Mother! Come and see my plant. It has roots on it!"

Sure enough! Little white roots were growing from the slip. "I'll put it in dirt right away," said Joyce.

"No, you must wait until the roots are longer and stronger," said her mother.

When the roots were stronger, Joyce filled a flower pot with dirt. She planted her geranium in the pot. She pressed the dirt around the roots. She was careful not to break the roots.

The little plant grew very well. One day Joyce found more buds on it. "My geranium is going to have flowers! I think they will be red flowers. The geranium in school had red flowers."

In a few days the buds opened. The flowers were red. They were just like the flowers on the plant at school.

Uncle Don told Joyce that new plants grow in different ways. "There are many ways of getting new plants. One way is to plant bulbs. We plant bulbs to get tulip plants. We also plant bulbs for narcissus plants. Another way is to plant seeds. We plant corn and bean seeds. We get a great many plants from seeds. Another way is to grow new plants from slips. Your geranium plant grew from a slip.

"Since plants grow so easily, we don't need to keep the poor ones. We should keep only the good strong ones. We keep the seeds from the best plants. We keep the best bulbs. We cut slips from the plants we like. That is the way we get the best kinds of plants. We should not plant seeds or bulbs from poor plants. Many men have spent their lives finding out how to raise the best kinds of plants."

Jimmy's Puppy

Jimmy wanted a dog. He thought a dog would be the very best pet he could have. But Jimmy's mother said, "You would have to feed it and keep it clean. You would have to train it. Jimmy, a dog is so much work. I don't believe you are old enough to care for one."

But Jimmy knew he could care for a dog. He decided he would save money enough to buy one of his own. He would show Mother that he could take care of a dog. All summer Jimmy earned money. He cut the grass. He pulled up vegetables for Mother. He washed dishes. He saved his money carefully, for he wanted a dog very, very much.

"Maybe I'll get some money for my birthday, too," thought Jimmy. "I'll put it with what I already have. Then I can buy a dog." He knew the kind of dog he wanted. He was going to buy a collie dog. He thought the collie dog the smartest kind of dog there was.

Jimmy's birthday came. He dressed and ran down to breakfast. He had always found his birthday present beside his breakfast plate. This time there was no present! Father and Mother did not say a word about Jimmy's birthday. For a moment Jimmy felt like crying. But he was a good sport. He did not cry.

After breakfast Father said, "Jimmy, I found something at our back door this morning. Will you come and see it?"

Jimmy was not happy as he went with Father. But then he began to smile. Sitting in a box near the door was the dearest softest little bundle of a dog that Jimmy had ever seen. Jimmy picked up the dog and held him tight.

"Oh, Father! Mother! Is he my own? My very own?"

Father and Mother nodded.

"Oh! I'm so happy! This is the best birthday present I've ever had!"

Jimmy looked at his roly-poly puppy. "And it's a collie!" he cried. "Just the very kind I wanted! I'm going to take him to school. I want the children to see him."

"You must take good care of him," said Mother. "A puppy must have good care. He can not take care of himself very well."

"I will ask Dick how to take care of him," said Jimmy. "Dick has two dogs. He knows how to take care of them."

At school the children gathered around Jimmy and his puppy. "He's a collie," said Jimmy proudly. "See how long his nose is."

"He's a pretty color," said Jane. "He has pretty red-brown hair."

"His hair is the color of copper," said Miss Parker.

"Copper! That's a good name for a dog," said Susan. "Jimmy, why don't you call him Copper?"

"I guess I will," said Jimmy. "I like Copper for a name."

"How soft his hair is," said Nancy.

"Yes, it is, but it isn't as soft as my cat's hair," said Susan. "My cat has very soft fine hair. My cat's hair was thick in winter. It got thick in autumn. Her hair kept her warm during winter. Is your dog's hair thick?"

Jimmy felt of his dog's hair. "Yes, it's thick. It's not so thick as it will be when Copper is grown."

"Feel of Copper's nose," said Dick. "Is it cold and wet?"

"Yes," said Jimmy.

"Then he is a healthy dog. If a dog has a warm, dry nose, he is sick. That is the way you can tell if your dog has a fever."

"Copper has sharp teeth!" said Jimmy. "Do cats have sharp teeth, Susan?"

"Yes, they do. My cat has sharp teeth. She can cut meat with her teeth," said Susan. "She can carry things in her mouth. She holds them with her teeth."

"Dogs use their teeth for tearing and cutting. They can tear meat," said Dick.

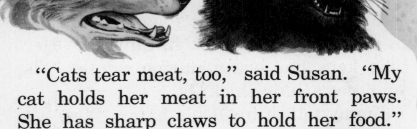

"Cats tear meat, too," said Susan. "My cat holds her meat in her front paws. She has sharp claws to hold her food."

"Dogs have sharp claws, too," said Jimmy. "You can hear Copper's claws when he walks on the floor."

"You can't hear a cat when it walks," said Susan. "A cat pulls its claws up between its toes when it walks. A cat can walk quietly because its claws do not touch the floor. A dog can not pull back its claws. A cat uses its claws to protect itself. It will scratch and fight with its claws."

"Dogs and cats are alike in some ways," said Dick. "They both hunt for food. But the way they hunt is not the same. Cats can see well at night. So cats hunt at night. Dogs can't see so well at night. But dogs can smell very well. Dogs use their noses more than their eyes when hunting.

"Cats can climb trees, but dogs can not. Cats are more graceful than dogs."

Dick told Jimmy the best things to do for his dog. Here they are:

To Care for a Collie Puppy

When it is very young, feed it milk.
When it is older, feed it cooked
  vegetables.
Feed it raw meat as its teeth grow.
Give it bones. The bones will keep its
  teeth clean. It can gnaw the bones.
Do not feed it bread or potatoes.
Be sure to feed it out of clean dishes.
Keep it out of doors as much as possible.
Always keep it clean.
When it is very young, do not bathe
  it. Brush it when it gets dirty.
  When it is older, wash it with warm
  water and soap.
Be sure it is dry before it goes outside.
Give it plenty of clean fresh water.
Have a clean bed for it to sleep in.

Here are some dogs and cats that children like.

My Cat

By Susan

I have a cat. Her name is Missy. She keeps herself clean. She licks her paws. She licks her hair. She drinks sweet milk. I feed her cooked meat and fish.

Missy does not eat birds. I do not let her chase the birds. I keep my cat in the house at night. I have a good clean bed for her to sleep in.

Missy has three kittens. They were born alive. They did not have their eyes open. Missy feeds them milk from her body. Kittens can not take care of themselves when they are very young. The mother cat takes care of them.

Missy's kittens will soon catch mice. I will keep them shut up at night. Cats see so well at night that they can see birds. My cats must not kill birds.

Dick's Cow

"Hey, Jimmy," called Dick. "Come over and see my cow."

"Is she a real one?" asked Jimmy, as he came running over.

Dick took Jimmy out to the barn. There was the cow. She was a big cow She was brown and white. She was eating hay.

"Where did you get her?" asked Jimmy.

"Dad bought her. He told me she would be my cow. Just think of all the milk we will have."

"I wish I had a cow," said Jimmy. "A cow would be lots of fun."

"You can come over and help me take care of my cow," said Dick. "We can feed her. We can take her out to pasture."

"Do you know how to milk her?" asked Jimmy.

"No, not yet," said Dick. "Dad milks her. But he is going to show me how to milk when I am bigger. You come over after supper and see how it's done."

Jimmy came over after supper. He went to the barn with Dick and his father. They took a clean pail. Dick's father sat on a stool. He put the pail between his knees. The boys watched him milk the cow. Soon the pail was full of milk. They took the milk to the house. They poured it through a clean cloth. They wanted to be sure the milk was clean. Dick's father filled a clean milk bottle with milk and gave it to Jimmy.

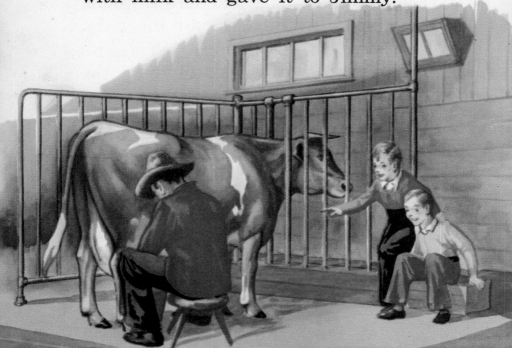

"Here is milk for your breakfast," he said. "It is good milk, and milk is good food. It helps make good teeth. It helps your bones grow. It will help make you strong."

Dick and his father poured the milk into clean bottles. They put the bottles into the ice box. "We will see what happens to the milk tonight," said Dick's father.

In the morning Dick looked at the bottles. "Oh! The milk has cream on it!" he cried.

"Yes," said Dick's mother. "When we let milk stand, the cream comes to the top. Now you can have cream for your oatmeal."

"I can have milk to drink, too," said Dick.

"Yes," said Mother, "but we will not take the cream off the milk you drink. Milk with the cream gone isn't as good food as milk with cream in it."

"What do you do with milk after the cream has been taken off?" asked Dick.

"We feed it to the chickens. Farmers sometimes feed it to pigs. I use it for cooking and sometimes I make cottage cheese."

"I like cottage cheese," said Dick. "Can we make some?"

"We will make some on Saturday. We must have sour milk first," said Mother.

Dick wanted to learn all he could about milk. "Why do you always put milk into clean bottles?" he asked.

"Because clean milk is good food," said Mother. "Dirty milk might make you sick. All food should be kept clean.

"Let's do an experiment. We'll put some milk into a clean bottle. Then we'll put some into a dirty bottle. We'll put both bottles into the ice box. We'll see what happens."

In two days Dick opened the bottles. The milk in the clean bottle was still sweet. It tasted good. The milk in the dirty bottle was sour. Dick made a face when he smelled it.

"Doesn't clean milk ever get sour?" asked Dick.

"Oh, yes, but not so soon as dirty milk," said Mother. "We can keep clean milk sweet in the ice box for many days."

"What happens if we don't keep milk in the ice box?" asked Dick.

"Let's see," said Mother. They put the two bottles on the kitchen table. They left them there two more days.

"Something is happening to the milk," said Dick.

"Yes," said Mother. "When milk sours, it makes a curd. You can see the curd in the bottles. Can you see the difference between the milk in the two bottles?"

"Oh, yes," cried Dick. "In the clean bottle the curd is more solid. It has all gone to the bottom of the bottle. I can see big holes in the curd in the dirty bottle."

"That is one way we can tell clean sour milk from dirty sour milk," said Mother.

"We'll save the clean sour milk for our cottage cheese," said Mother. "On Saturday we'll make some butter, too."

"Butter!" said Dick. "How do you make butter?"

"We make butter from cream," said Mother. "On Saturday we will have lots of cream."

Dick could hardly wait for Saturday to come. On Saturday morning he was up early. After breakfast Mother put some cream into a jar. She put a beater into the jar.

Dick turned the handle. He watched the cream through the glass. Soon some pieces of butter came to the top! Mother helped Dick take the butter out. She put it into a dish. She pressed it down with a spoon until all of the milk was

gone.   Mother put some salt into the butter. She mixed the salt all through the butter.

Dick ate some of it. It tasted good. He spread some of it on bread. Um-m-m! It was good!

"You have made something else, too," said Mother. "This jar was full of cream. Now it is full of buttermilk. Bring a glass. You can drink it."

Dick brought a glass. He filled it with buttermilk. Dick liked it. "Buttermilk is good!" he said.

"We will try another experiment," said Mother. "Put some of the butter into a pan. Put the pan on the stove."

Dick tried it. Soon the butter melted. "It looks like fat," cried Dick.

"It is fat," said Mother. "Fat helps make milk a good food."

"I'm glad we have a cow," said Dick. "I know now why we take care of cows and feed them. Cows give us some of our very best food. Milk, cream, butter, and buttermilk are all good foods."

"That's right," said Mother. "Babies are fed on milk as soon as they are born. They get milk from their mothers. Sometimes babies drink milk from a bottle. But all babies live on milk."

"Oh, I almost forgot the cottage cheese," said Dick. "Can we make it now?"

"Yes, we can make it right now," said Mother. "Here is our clean sour milk."

Mother put the sour milk into a pan. She put the pan on the stove. When the milk was hot something happened to it.

"I can see the cheese," cried Dick.

"Yes," said Mother, "and what is left is called *whey*. It has no cream in it. It has no curds. Most of it is water."

Mother poured the cottage cheese and whey out of the pan. She poured them through a piece of cheesecloth. All the whey went through. The cottage cheese was on the cheesecloth. Dick made the cheese into balls. That was the way he liked cottage cheese.

Dick told Miss Parker and the children all about the cow. He told them about

milk. He told them about the experiments he and his mother had done.

"Can't we try some of Dick's experiments in school?" asked Jane. "We can
buy some milk."

"I'll bring you some milk," said Dick.

The next morning Dick brought some
milk to school. The children had fun
with the milk. First they had milk. Then
they had cream. They made butter. They
made cottage cheese. They learned all
about milk. They learned these things:

Milk is good food.

Cream is good food.

Butter is good food.

Cottage cheese is good food.

Bob Goes to the Store

Bob had a new wagon. It was red and black. It had red wheels. Bob liked to play with his wagon.

One Saturday morning Bob's mother said, "Bob, will you go to the store for me? I am too busy to go."

"Oh, yes," said Bob. "I'll take my new wagon."

"That will be fine," said Mother. "I want you to buy many things for me. Here is a list of things for you to buy. You may go to Mr. Gray's store. He will help you."

This is the list Bob's mother gave him:

One dozen eggs
One pound of butter
One quart of milk
One dozen oranges
Some other fruit
Meat for dinner
Two vegetables

Mr. Gray was glad to see Bob. "What do you want this morning?" he asked.

"Mother gave me a list," said Bob. "I will put the things in my wagon. First, I want a dozen eggs. Are they fresh?"

"Yes, they came from the farm this morning," said Mr. Gray. "Here they are. Put them where they will not break."

"Then I want a pound of butter," said Bob. "I want a quart of milk, too."

"The milk is fresh," said Mr. Gray. "So is the butter. The milk just came. It is in a clean bottle. The bottle has a top on it. The butter is in a tight package. It will keep clean."

"That's good," said Bob. "Mother says food must always be kept clean. Dirty food might make us sick. Now I want a dozen oranges and some other fruit."

"Here are the oranges. They came here by train. They grow where it is warm," said Mr. Gray. "We have many other fruits today. Which kind do you want?"

"I think I'll take some apples," said Bob. "I like apples."

"Apples are good food," said Mr. Gray. "An apple a day keeps the doctor away!"

Bob laughed. He had heard that before.

"I always wash apples before I eat them," he said. "I peel oranges."

"That's good," said Mr. Gray. "All fruit should be washed or peeled."

"I have two more things on my list," said Bob. "Meat and vegetables. Mother said I might choose the kind I like."

"We have many kinds of meat," said Mr. Gray. "Which kind would you like?"

"I will take some beef," said Bob. "I like roast beef. Mother says it is good food to help make boys grow."

"Now, what vegetables do you want?" asked Mr. Gray.

It was hard for Bob to decide. He liked all kinds of vegetables. At last he said he would take carrots and beans.

"You will have a fine dinner," said Mr. Gray. "Can you get all those things home?"

"I will be careful," said Bob. "I will look both ways before I cross a street."

When Bob got home, Mother looked at the things he had bought. She was pleased. Bob had done very well.

"The eggs, milk, beans, and butter will help build good teeth and bones," said Mother. "The milk, beef, eggs, and vegetables will help make you strong. The oranges and apples are good foods to keep you well. I think I will send you to the store often."

Pictures in Rocks

One morning the children saw a big rock on Miss Parker's desk.

"That's a funny rock," said Jimmy. "It has shells all over it."

"Where did you get it?" Dick asked.

"A man gave it to me," said Miss Parker.

By this time the other children were trying to see the rock.

"Where did the man find it?" asked Bob.

"Quite near here," said Miss Parker.

"Where did the shells come from?" asked Jane.

"If you'll sit down, I'll tell you about it." Miss Parker held the rock so all the children could see it. "You said it had shells on it, Jimmy. Look closely. Do they look just like shells?"

Jimmy looked. He tried to pick one of the shells from the rock. "No," he said. "I can't pick it off the way I could if it were a shell."

"What does it look like?" asked Miss Parker.

"Something like hard mud," said Jimmy.

"It *is* something like hard mud," said Miss Parker. "These are not really shells that you see in the rock. They are just the prints of shells. Have you ever seen shells that look like these?"

"Yes," said Susan. "I found some at the seashore last summer."

"I found some at the lake," said Bob. "They were clam shells. Once I found live clams in the water near the shore."

"These prints were made by little animals something like clams," said Miss Parker. "They lived many, many years ago. When they died, they were covered with mud. The mud got harder and harder until it made this rock. The shells went to pieces. Only their prints are left. Now we call these prints *fossils*."

"I saw some fossils at a museum once," said Jimmy. "But they were big ones. One of them was as big as this room!"

"Those were fossils of some of the largest animals that ever lived," said Miss Parker. "We call the bones or prints of animals that lived years ago, fossils. Sometimes we find the prints of plants in rocks. They are fossils, too.

Fossils tell us about animals and plants that lived long ago on the earth."

"I'd like to find a fossil," said Bob.

"Perhaps you can," said Miss Parker. "Would you like to go on a field trip to look for fossils?"

The children wanted to go. Miss Parker told them to wear old clothes the next day. She asked them to bring small bags to carry any fossils they might find.

The next morning Miss Parker and the children went to a place where there were fossils. The children hunted in the rocks for fossils.

"Oh, here's a fossil just like the ones in your rock!" shouted Bob. He ran to show Miss Parker. His fossil was almost like a shell.

"The rock was broken, and this fossil fell out," said Miss Parker.

Soon all the children were running to show Miss Parker what they had found.

Nancy had a fossil that looked like this.

Susan had one that looked like this.

Jimmy's fossil looked like this.

"This is the best field trip we've ever had," said Jane, as they took their fossils back to school.

Rocks Have Names

After the trip for fossils, the children brought many interesting rocks to school. They decided to make some shelves for the most interesting ones.

The children soon learned that some of their rocks were not as hard as others. Most of the rocks with fossils in them were not very hard. They could be broken easily.

Miss Parker told them, "Many fossils are found in limestone. I will show you how to tell limestone from other rocks. Limestone is often a gray color. It is so soft that it can easily be scratched with a penny. But I like to be sure, and so I experiment with the rocks I find. This is the way I do it.

"I have here a small bottle of acid. I will put a drop of acid on this rock. If the acid makes bubbles, the rock is limestone. If it doesn't make bubbles, it is not limestone." Miss Parker put some acid on the rock.

"Look!" the children cried. "The acid makes bubbles. This is limestone!"

The children filled a shelf with rocks that they found to be limestone. Some of the limestone had fossils in it. They put these at one end of the shelf. They wrote *Limestone with fossils*. They put the limestone without fossils at the other end of the shelf. They wrote *Limestone without fossils*.

Some of the rocks the children found felt like sand. They could rub grains of sand off these rocks. Miss Parker told them that these rocks were sandstone. Some of the sandstone was red, some was yellow, and some was brown.

"Sandstone is pretty," said Nancy.

The children put their sandstone on two shelves. They wrote *Red Sandstone, Yellow Sandstone, Brown Sandstone,* and *Gray Sandstone* underneath the rocks. They found fossils in some of the sandstone.

"Sandstone has hard grains of sand in it," said Bob. "I scratched my hand on a piece of sandstone."

"Yes," said Miss Parker. "Those grains are hard enough to scratch glass."

"Let's see if they will," said Susan.

Miss Parker gave Susan a glass jar. Susan rubbed it with a piece of sandstone. The sandstone did scratch the glass.

"That is why we have to be careful when we clean our aquarium," said Jane. "If we rub the sand against the glass, it will scratch the glass."

Another kind of rock that the children found was gray and smooth. It was in layers. When it broke, it broke in layers. Some of it had fossils in it.

"It looks like limestone," said Bob. But when he put the acid on it, it didn't make bubbles. It was not limestone.

RED SANDSTONE

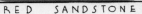

YELLOW SANDSTONE

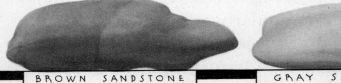

BROWN SANDSTONE

GRAY SANDSTONE

"This is shale," said Miss Parker.

"Something comes off on my fingers," said Nancy.

"Smell the shale," said Miss Parker.

"It smells like mud!" said Bob.

"It smells like clay. In art class we made dishes out of clay," said Jane.

"That's what shale is made of," said Miss Parker. "Shale is made of clay."

"Sandstone is made of sand," said Jimmy. "And limestone is made of shells."

"Some of it is," said Miss Parker.

"And don't forget the fossils we sometimes find in rocks," said Dick.

SHALE

LIMESTONE WITH FOSSILS

LIMESTONE WITHOUT FOSSILS

How Soil Is Made

The children found some rocks that were falling to pieces. One piece of sandstone was so soft they could break it in their hands.

"It's just like sand," said Susan.

"Yes," said Miss Parker. "When sandstone breaks up, it makes sand."

"What makes rocks break?" asked Bob.

"Several things may happen to them," said Miss Parker. "Do you remember the experiment you tried by freezing water?"

"Do you mean when we froze some water in a bottle?" asked Jane.

"Yes. What happened to the bottle?"

"It broke," said Susan.

"The same thing may happen to rocks. Water gets into tiny cracks in the rocks and freezes. When water freezes, it expands. It pushes the rocks apart and breaks them just as the ice broke the bottle. Have you seen how sidewalks break in winter? Water freezes in the cracks and pushes the sidewalk apart."

"The water froze in the pipes in our house last winter and broke them," said Jimmy.

"Water often breaks things when it freezes," said Miss Parker. "Something else helps break rocks—the sun helps."

"How?" asked the children.

"What do we get from the sun?" asked Miss Parker.

"Light and heat," they answered.

"The heat breaks the rocks," said Miss Parker. "Did you ever make a camp fire between rocks?"

"I've seen my brother do that," said Nancy.

"Did anything happen to the rocks when they got hot?" asked Miss Parker.

"Yes," said Nancy. "They broke."

"That's right," said Miss Parker. "That's because part of the rock got hot faster than the rest. A dish will break if you set it on a hot stove. It gets hot too fast. The sun doesn't heat the rocks as fast as fire does, but it helps break them in much the same way. Rivers

help break rocks, too. Rivers push rocks
along. The rocks strike other rocks and
break. Sometimes the wind blows sand
against rocks and helps break them. There
are many ways that rocks are broken."

"When we went to the mountains last
summer, we saw a big rock that was being
broken up," said Bob. "A tree was growing right out of it and making a crack
deeper and deeper in it. Dad said perhaps
a bird carried a seed to the rock and
dropped it in a little crack. The roots
grew and grew. As they grew, they pushed
into the crack and made it bigger."

"Many plants help break up rocks,"
said Miss Parker. "When rocks are brok-
en, they make soil. Some rocks make
sand when they are broken. Some
rocks make clay. It takes many, many
years for rocks to change into soil."

We Need Soil

"If there were no soil, we wouldn't be alive," said Miss Parker.

"Why?" asked the children.

"Because to live we must have plants. Plants can not grow without soil."

"Why do we need plants?" asked Jane. "We could eat meat. Meat comes from animals. Beef comes from cattle."

"But cattle eat grass," Bob said. "And grass is a plant."

"Yes," said Miss Parker. "We would soon be hungry if all the plants died. And plants must have soil to live."

"Some plants live in water," said Susan.

"But many of them have their roots in the soil at the bottom of the water. Don't you remember that you planted the water plants in the soil of your aquarium?"

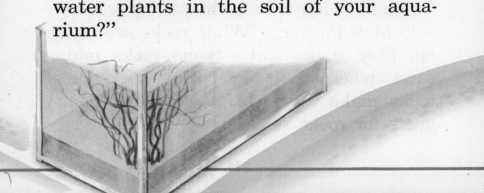

"Trees, garden plants, and grass all grow in soil," Miss Parker went on. "They have roots that go down into the ground. The roots get water from the soil. The plants also use part of the soil. We say that plants use minerals from the soil to help them grow. Rocks are made of minerals. Soil is made of broken up rocks. That is how soil happens to have minerals in it."

"That is a new word," said Jane.

Miss Parker wrote the word *mineral* on the blackboard. Under it she wrote,

Plants use minerals from the soil.

"Some minerals are hard," said Miss Parker. "Some are soft. Some dissolve in water. The plants use the minerals that dissolve in water."

"There are several kinds of soil," Miss Parker went on. "Some soil is made of broken up sandstone."

"That is sand," said Jimmy.

"Yes, and some soil is clay," said Miss Parker. "There is another kind of soil that you should know about. It is made of dead plants that have decayed. We call that kind of soil *humus*. Humus makes garden soil darker than sand. Sometimes humus soil is almost black. We often find little pieces of sticks and roots in humus."

"My dad calls it leaf mold," said Dick. "In autumn he puts all the dead leaves from the yard in a big hole."

"When all the leaves have decayed, they make leaf mold or humus," said Miss Parker. "What does your father do with the humus?"

"He puts it around the rose bushes," said Dick.

"The humus will help make the roses grow," said Miss Parker. "The rain will go down through the humus and dissolve part of it. The roots of the rose bushes can use the part that dissolves."

"Earthworms help make humus," Miss Parker went on. "Earthworms eat dead leaves. The leaves go into the earthworm's body. The earthworm's body uses part of the leaves. The rest comes out and is left in the soil. The soil is then much finer than when the earthworm ate it. The water can dissolve part of the soil. It can go into the roots of live plants. The plants use it for food."

"That's why earthworms help the farmer, isn't it?" asked Jimmy.

"Yes," answered Miss Parker. "Then there is still another kind of soil. It is made of sand and clay and humus all mixed together."

"What's the name of that soil?" asked Dick.

"We call it *loam*," said Miss Parker. "Would you like to try an experiment with soils?"

"Oh, yes," the children said. They always liked to try experiments.

This is what the children did.
1. They filled two flower pots with sand.

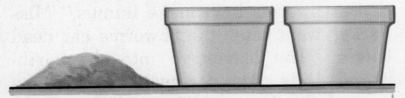

2. They filled two flower pots with clay.

3. They filled two flower pots with humus.

4. They mixed some sand, clay, and humus to make loam.
5. They filled two flower pots with loam.

Miss Parker gave the children some corn and some beans. They planted the corn and beans in their pots of soil.

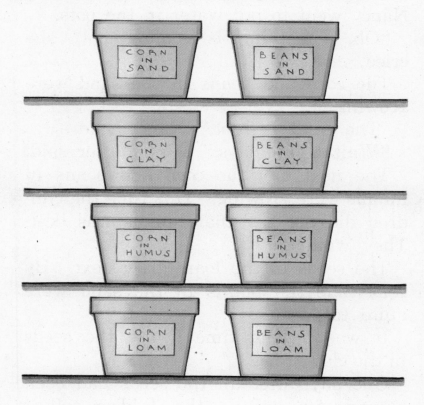

They put all the pots in the window. "They'll get sunshine here," said Bob.

"We'll water them every day," said Jimmy.

The children looked each day to see if
their seeds were growing. Nothing happened for several days. Then one morning
Nancy went to put water in the pots.

"Oh, something is coming up!" she
cried.

The corn and beans in the sand were
growing.

"The sand is best," Nancy said.

"Wait a few days," Miss Parker said.

The next day the corn and beans in
humus were growing. This time the children did not say that humus was best.
They waited.

The seeds in the loam grew next. By
that time the plants in the sand were
quite tall.

It was a long time before the seeds
in the clay grew.

One day, after all the seeds had been
growing for a while, the children talked
about them.

"The plants in the sand aren't growing
so well now," said Dick. "The ones in the
humus aren't growing very well, either."

"The plants in the sand and the humus came up first," said Susan. "Why haven't they grown as well as the ones in loam?"

"The ones in the sand grew quickly because you gave them plenty of water," said Miss Parker. "Sand doesn't stick together and the water can get to the seeds easily. The little plants could grow quickly and push through the soil. You know there is some food in the seeds. After that was all gone, there wasn't any food in the sand to make the plants grow any more. The plants stopped growing. The plants in the humus grew fast at first because humus is warmer than the other soils."

"Clay sticks together," said Bob. "Is that why the seeds took so long to grow in it?"

"Yes," said Miss Parker. "The water couldn't get to the seeds as fast as in the other soils. After the seeds began to grow, the roots couldn't get air. It was hard for the little plants to push through the clay."

"Loam has enough sand in it to let water and air in easily," said Jimmy. "It has enough clay to hold the water. It has enough humus to make it rich enough for the plants. Most plants grow best in loam."

"That is right," said Miss Parker. "Some plants grow better in loam with more sand than clay. Some grow best in loam that has more clay than sand. And some plants need very rich soil. Rich soil has more humus than sand or clay. Farmers have to know what kinds of soils are best for the plants they are raising."

"Let's plant our beans and corn out of doors," said Susan.

"That's a good plan," said Miss Parker. "We will take them to the school garden where all the plants will have loam."

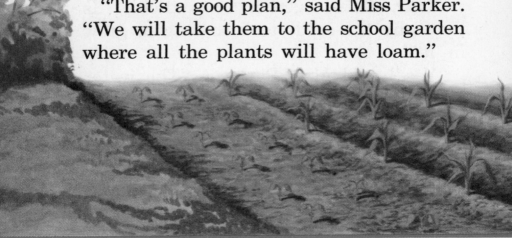

How Soil Is Carried

Miss Parker had promised to take the children for a field trip. When they came to school, the sky looked dark.

"I think it's going to rain," said Nancy. "The sky is full of dark clouds."

"Oh, dear," cried Susan. "Then we can't go on our trip."

In a few minutes big drops were coming fast. The children looked so unhappy that Miss Parker laughed. "It's just a shower," she said. "See, the sun is already showing through the clouds. Perhaps the rain will stop soon. Then we can go."

Miss Parker was right. In just a few minutes the rain was over and the children started on their trip.

The water was running down the walks. It was running down the roads. "What a lot of water," said Bob. "Look! There is a little river going down the hill."

"The water is making a ditch in the sand," said Jimmy.

The children watched the water run down the hill. The ditch grew wider.

At the bottom of the hill they found sand that the water had dropped.

"That is the way big rivers make their beds," said Miss Parker. "A river often begins as a little stream. The stream washes away the sand and makes a larger ditch. This little stream has made a ditch. The water carries soil as it flows along. It carries more soil when it is flowing fast. It carries less soil when it is flowing slowly. Where did this little stream make the deepest ditch?"

"Where the hill is steep," said Nancy.

"Yes," said Miss Parker. "When the water came down on the level ground, what happened?"

"It spread out," said Dick.

"It dropped some sand," said Susan.

"That's what happens to the little streams that make larger streams. When they are flowing fast, they make deep, narrow beds. When they flow more slowly, they get wider and not so deep," said Miss Parker. "This is one way that soil is carried from place to place."

"I know another way soil is carried," said Jimmy. "The wind carries soil when it blows hard. Sometimes we have dust storms."

"Yes," said Miss Parker. "There are places where so much soil is blown that it sometimes covers fences. Soil is carried from place to place in many ways. It never stays in one place very long. This hill may be all washed away some day. Then it will be flat where we now are."

Jimmy Learns About His Skin

Jimmy had been playing ball. The day was hot. And Jimmy was hot. "See how I sweat," he said. "I'm wet all over. Where does the water come from?"

"Maybe it comes out of the air," said Nancy. "You know water does come out of the air."

"This water didn't come out of the air," said Jimmy. "Cold brings water out of the air. I'm very hot."

"Jimmy is right," said Miss Parker. "This water didn't come out of the air."

"Maybe it came through my skin," laughed Jimmy. "There must be holes in my skin." All of the children laughed.

"Maybe Jimmy is right," said Miss Parker. "Let's look at his skin."

"Let's use the reading glass," said Nancy. "If there are holes, they must be very small." Nancy looked first. "There *are* some openings," she said.

"Does water come out of my body through those openings?" asked Jimmy.

"Yes, it does," said Miss Parker. "You can see it come out if you look closely. Sometimes the water comes out slowly and evaporates. When you are hot, the water comes out so fast it can't evaporate. We call the water that comes out of the openings *sweat*.

"Oil comes out of some of the openings, too," Miss Parker went on. "The oil helps keep the skin soft. When your skin is dirty, the openings get filled up. Then oil can not come out. When you take a bath, you make your skin clean. When the skin is clean, the oil can come out."

"If there are openings in my skin, why doesn't water run into my body through them?" asked Jimmy.

"They are made so water can come out but can't go in," Miss Parker explained.

The Cardinal's Family

One bright morning late in March Dick heard a whistle. It came from the yard. He ran to the door. He thought it was one of the boys. No one was there but the whistle came loud and clear. It sounded like a boy whistling to a dog. But no boy was in sight.

Dick stood at the door. He called, "Bob! Jimmy!" No one answered. All at once he saw a bright red flash. A red bird flew to the top of a spruce tree.

"Oh, Mother!" cried Dick. "There is a cardinal in the yard. I heard it whistle! Then I saw it in the spruce tree!"

Mother came. She and Dick watched the cardinal. It sat on top of the spruce tree and sang.

In a few minutes it flew to another tree. It sang again. Then it flew to another tree and sang again. How its feathers shone in the sun!

"That is a male bird," said Mother. "He must be choosing his territory."

"What does that mean?" asked Dick.

"The male cardinal finds a good place for a nest. He wants all other male cardinals to stay away. We call the place he finds his territory."

"It wouldn't take all that space for a nest," said Dick.

"No," laughed Mother. "Perhaps he needs space for a nest and a yard, too. The male cardinal picks out his territory before he gets a mate."

Just then something happened in the spruce tree. Another male cardinal flew to the tree.

Whir-r-r! went their wings and the two birds came down to the ground. Such a noise the birds made as they flew at each other. Such a mixing of red feathers!

"They're fighting," cried Dick.

Then one bird flew away and the other came back to the tree. He smoothed his feathers. He raised his crest and sang.

Mother laughed. "It's just as if he were saying, 'Stay out of my territory.' "

"What was the matter?" asked Dick.

"The male cardinal had chosen this place for his territory and when another male cardinal came, he wanted to drive it away," said Mother.

"How do you know which bird won?" asked Dick. "They looked alike to me."

"I don't know," said Mother. "But one of them won, that's sure!"

Several days later Dick saw another bird with the cardinal. This bird was the same size and shape but not so red. In fact, it was hardly red at all. It was almost brown. It had a crest with red tips. Its tail had red tips, too.

"Look, Mother," said Dick. "There is a bird with the cardinal and they aren't fighting."

"That is a female cardinal," said Mother. "Perhaps our cardinal has a mate."

Dick watched the birds. The male would fly to a branch near the female and sing. Sometimes she would fly away. Then he would follow her. Sometimes she would sing. But the two birds stayed near each other in the yard.

One day Dick saw the female cardinal carrying a small twig. She flew to the spruce tree. The male followed and sang from the top of the tree. When the female came out and flew away, he followed her.

"I think the cardinals are building a nest," Dick told Mother.

"Then we must be careful not to frighten them," she said.

Every day Dick watched. Sometimes he saw the female carrying small twigs. Once he saw her carrying a piece of paper.

"The male cardinal doesn't help," said Dick. "He just sings while she works."

For about two weeks Dick watched the female cardinal work. He watched the male cardinal, too. Then he didn't see them for a few days. He wondered if something had happened to the birds.

"Birds sometimes leave their nest for a few days after it is built," Father told him. "I think the cardinals will be back."

Father was right. The next morning Dick heard a cheerful whistle. He jumped out of bed. He ran to the window. There was the male cardinal on the very tip of the spruce tree. And below him through the branches Dick could see the female cardinal's beak.

Dick was excited. He could see the nest from the window.

"I will get the field glasses," said Father. "Then we can see better."

With the field glasses Dick could see the female bird quite well. She was on the nest. The nest was close to the trunk of the tree.

Every day Dick watched the birds. Sometimes the female would leave the nest. Then Dick could see the eggs. He wasn't sure how many there were. He and Father looked in a bird book. The book said cardinals lay three or four speckled eggs.

The male bird always followed the female bird when she left the nest. He would come back first and fly to a branch near the nest. He would make a noise that sounded like "chip." The female would answer "chip." Then she would fly to the nest and sit on the eggs.

One day Dick saw the male taking a big green caterpillar to the nest.

"It must be time for the eggs to hatch," said Father. "Or perhaps the caterpillar is for the female bird."

The next morning both birds were gone. Dick watched a long while. At last the male came with a caterpillar. Three open mouths came up from the nest.

"The eggs have hatched!" cried Dick. "Three baby birds! Aren't they funny!

They have no feathers. Their eyes aren't open. They don't look like cardinals."

"Wait a while," said Father.

How the male and female worked feeding their babies! Every day the three little cardinals grew. Their eyes opened. Their feathers began to grow. Soon they were pushing each other when they saw food.

At last they were so big the nest was too small to hold them. Dick saw one sitting on the edge of the nest. "Look out, you'll fall," he called. But the baby bird just opened its mouth for the next caterpillar.

Then all three baby birds were on the ground. They followed the old birds. They begged for food.

"The baby birds look like their mother," said Dick. "All of them must be females."

"All cardinals look alike when they are young," said Father. "The first feathers of many young birds are like those of their mother. After a while the baby cardinals will lose these feathers and grow new ones. Then the male birds will be red. The color they are now is more like the color of the leaves and bark of the tree. Their color helps protect the birds when they are in the nest. Red feathers would be seen easily by enemies."

"I hope a cat doesn't get them now," said Dick. "They can't fly very well."

"Cats catch many young birds when they first leave the nest," said Father. "That's why people should shut up their cats at night. Cats hunt more at night than in the day."

"The cardinals are the most beautiful birds we have had in our yard," said Dick. "Perhaps they'll come again next year."

House for Rent

As spring came, Dick watched other birds come back. He kept a record of new birds he saw every day.

Dick thought it would be fun to build a bird house. His father helped him make one. They made a house of little logs. Dick put it on top of a high post. Its front door was a small round hole. The hole was just big enough for a small bird to go through it.

"It looks like a house for rent," said Susan who had come over to see the new bird house. "It's waiting for a family of birds to move into it."

"The birds are coming back from the south," said Father. "Maybe some of them will choose this house to live in."

"We will watch every day," said Dick.

In a few days two bluebirds had come
to live in the house.

"Goody!" laughed Susan. "There'll be
a family of bluebirds. And they are such
pretty birds!"

"Bluebirds look something like robins,
don't they?" asked Dick.

"Yes, people used to call them blue robins," said Father. "They belong to the same family as the robins. They used to build nests in hollow trees. But now they build nests in houses like this wherever they can find one. In the summer bluebirds often live in orchards."

As soon as the bluebirds had found the bird house, the female began to build a nest in it. She carried dry grass to the house. She tucked it away in the house until she had a soft place for her eggs.

Several days later Dick's father held Susan on his shoulder. She looked through the little hole. "Oh! I see something!" she cried. "The female bluebird has laid an egg. It is pale blue."

The female laid four eggs. Then she did not leave her nest. Her mate flew

in and out of the house bringing her food. Dick and Susan watched every day to see what was happening.

One day Dick said, "There should be baby birds today."

But what a sad thing had happened! There on the ground were scattered bits of blue feathers. And flying around the bird house was the male bluebird. He was making sad little calls.

"His mate must have been killed," cried Dick.

"Oh!" cried Susan. "Something got into the nest. It ate up the mother bird!"

"Maybe it was a cat," said Father.

Dick's father held Susan on his shoulder and let her look through the hole. "The nest is empty," she said. "Whatever ate the mother bird must have eaten the eggs, too. Oh, dear!"

"Cats can climb up to this bird house too easily," said Father. "I know what we can do. We'll get some tin. We'll put it around the post. We will make a collar for the post. The cat can't climb over a tin collar. Then another female bluebird can lay her eggs in there. She and her eggs will be safe."

The children put the tin collar around the post near the house. Then they watched again.

Soon the male bluebird found another mate. He brought her to the bird house. She made a new nest. In a few days there were some pale blue eggs in the nest.

Dick and Susan watched the bird house every day. The mother bluebird was on the nest. "The old cat can't get her now," said Dick. "The tin collar will keep cats away."

The eggs hatched. Then there were four baby birds in the nest. The father and mother bluebirds were very busy. They had to feed their babies. And they were such hungry babies!

Dick and Susan watched the father and mother birds bring insects for their babies. They kept a record of the trips the birds made in one hour. This is what they wrote.

Number of times the female came to the nest with an insect in her mouth: *4 times*.

Number of times the male came to the nest with an insect in his mouth: *3 times*.

The babies always had their mouths open. "They are always ready for more food," laughed Dick.

"Why do the big birds always carry something away from the nest when they go?" asked Susan.

"They are cleaning the nest," said Dick's father. "They must keep the nest clean as well as feed the birds. They are always busy."

The baby birds grew larger. Their feathers grew. The feathers on their backs looked gray. Their breasts were speckled. Soon they could fly a little.

For a few days the babies flew with their father and mother. But soon they were old enough to live by themselves. They could get their own food. They could hide from cats. They could take care of themselves.

Soon there was another family of blue-birds in the bird house. "I guess this bird house is a good one," said Dick. "It always has birds in it."

A Box Full of Silkworms

By Jane

Science is fun. I like to experiment. We find out so many interesting things. But the most fun I ever had in science was with my silkworms.

Last spring our science teacher showed us some tiny eggs. Each egg was about as big as the head of a pin. We put them in a warm place in our schoolroom.

One day at play time it was raining. We were playing inside. Dick was looking at the worms. "Look!" he cried, "Something is coming out of our eggs."

Yes, some wiggling things were coming out of the eggs. They were very small.

"What are they, Miss Parker?" we cried.

"What do you think they are?" asked Miss Parker.

"Worms," said Dick.

"Caterpillars," said Jimmy.

"They are called silkworms," said Miss Parker. "They are really caterpillars."

"Do caterpillars like these make silk?" asked Nancy. "Was my silk dress made by silkworms?"

"Yes," said Miss Parker. "If we feed these caterpillars, they will grow. They will make silk."

"We must feed them," said Susan. "What will they eat?"

"They eat white mulberry leaves," said Miss Parker. So Dick found a white mulberry tree and brought some leaves.

I wanted some of the worms for my own. I asked Miss Parker if I might have some. She took a small box and put some mulberry leaves in it. She put about fifty little worms on the leaves.

Then she said, "You may have these. Be sure to feed them lots of mulberry leaves."

The silkworms lived on our back porch. They were always hungry. It was hard work finding mulberry leaves for them. The only mulberry tree I could find was quite a ways from home. Every day or two I rode on my bicycle to the tree. I picked a bag full of mulberry leaves.

My! How the silkworms grew! In a few days they filled the little box. Then I had to get a bigger box for them. Soon I had to get another big box. Half of them filled each big box.

They grew and grew!

Some were white caterpillars. Some of them were white with black stripes.

One day I was sad. Some of my silkworms looked sick. So I picked them out of the big boxes. I put them all by themselves in a little box. But they wouldn't eat. They were there all day.

When I came home from school, all of my worms looked sick. Not one was eating. I didn't go on my bicycle for more mulberry leaves. Maybe they would all die. They still looked sick when I went to bed.

The next morning I went out to see them. They were not sick. They were

shedding their skins! Most of them were out of their skins. They were busy eating. The others were part way out of their skins. Soon they were out. Then they started eating and growing again. I started getting more mulberry leaves for them.

Every one of my silkworms crawled out of its skin. Not only once but four times! And every time the worms stopped eating, I had a day of rest.

For six weeks I carried mulberry leaves to my big family. They grew until they were as big as my largest finger. I don't know why they are called worms. They are really not worms at all. They are caterpillars.

I watched them every day. It was fun to sit by the boxes and watch them eat.

The big surprise came one morning. I went out to look at my silkworms before breakfast. I took the cover from one of the boxes. There on the side of the box near the top was a cocoon. It was round and yellow. It was about one and one-half inches long. It was shaped like a robin's egg.

"Daddy! Mother! Oh, look!" was all I could say.

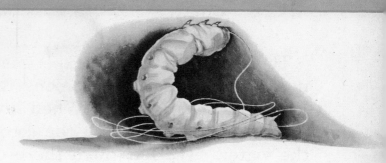

"Now you will have some silk," said Mother.

"They have stopped eating," said Dad.

Sure enough! The caterpillars had stopped eating.

"No more trips on my bicycle for mulberry leaves!" I said. I was glad those trips were over. The mulberry leaves were almost gone, too.

Some of the caterpillars were busy spinning. A little thread was coming from each head. They moved their heads back and forth. They looked so funny they made me laugh. Thread after thread was wound about the body of the caterpillar. At last the body was all covered up. The silkworm had made its silk.

In a few days all the caterpillars had spun cocoons. I had a box full of them.

The best part of the experiment came next day. I took my cocoons to school. We heated some water. When it was boiling, we dropped some of the cocoons into the water. We left them there until the caterpillar inside the cocoon was dead. Then we found the end of the silk thread and unwound it. We unwound and unwound! I thought we would never come to the end of it.

"Just think," said Susan. "One caterpillar made all of that silk. There is enough to reach up and down our schoolroom twenty times!"

"It takes a great many silkworms to make a silk dress," said Nancy.

"And it takes a great many mulberry leaves to feed them," said Miss Parker. "I guess Jane knows all about that."

We saved some of the cocoons. We left them in our schoolroom. In ten days moths hatched from the cocoons. They were small and white. They found mates. The female moths laid eggs. They laid a great many eggs. Then they died. The males died, too.

We looked at the eggs. They were just like the eggs we started with. We put them in a cold place. Next spring we will bring them out and put them in a warm place. Then some more silkworms will hatch. I'm sure they will be hungry. I had fun raising my silkworms. But next spring someone else may have the fun of feeding them and watching them grow.

Insect Catchers

Dick and Susan saw some birds flying in and out of the barn back of Dick's house. The birds had blue backs and brown breasts. They were darker than the bluebirds. They had long tails.

"They are barn swallows," said Dick. "They come every year. Dad says they are good birds to have in our yard. They catch insects."

"How graceful they are," said Susan. "Look how they turn!"

"Maybe they have a nest in the barn," said Dick. "Let's look."

Dick and Susan found a nest. It was high up. It was like the one they had seen last autumn on Bob's garage.

"It's made of mud," said Susan. "It's stuck to the wall. It has straw in it, too. The straw is stuck together with mud."

Dick got a ladder. Susan climbed up the ladder and looked into the nest. Then Dick climbed up and looked.

The inside of the nest was like a cup. It was lined with soft feathers.

"Let's watch and see what kind of eggs the barn swallow lays," said Dick.

A few days later, when Dick looked, he saw four little speckled white eggs in the mud nest. After that Susan climbed up every day to see if the eggs had hatched.

At last one day when they climbed up the ladder, they saw four baby birds in the nest.

"Let's hide," said Dick. "Then we can watch the mother swallow feed her babies."

Into the barn flew the female with something in her mouth. How fast one of the babies ate it!

Right behind her came the male with something for another baby mouth. Away they flew and back they came again and again with food for the hungry baby swallows. For days they fed the baby birds. They always brought insects. Swallows can catch insects as they fly.

One day the babies were big enough to leave the nest. The mother and father swallows pushed the babies out of the nest. The babies fell on some hay, and there they sat. They would not move. Their father and mother called and called to them. But they would not move an inch! They stayed there all night and all the next day.

Then the mother came to the barn with an insect in her mouth. She gave a soft little call. She showed the insect to the babies. The babies were so hungry they couldn't help going after the food.

At last the mother got the babies to fly a little. One by one they flew to a tree. Their parents flew around them. They chitter-chattered to them as much as to say, "Be careful. But don't be afraid. You'll soon learn to fly!" The parents stayed very near their babies until every baby was strong enough to fly.

When the last swallow flew away, Susan said, "Now we have four more swallows to eat up insects."

Spring Wild Flowers

The children often brought wild flowers to school. They always gave the flowers to Miss Parker, for she liked flowers very much.

"I like the first spring flowers almost better than any other flowers," she said. "Do you know the names of these wild flowers?"

"Violets and spring beauties and. . . " the children could not name the other wild flowers.

"I think we should know the names of the flowers that grow in the woods," said Jane. "Will you tell us their names, Miss Parker?"

"Yes, indeed," said Miss Parker.

"And please tell us something about the wild flowers," said Nancy. "Something interesting."

"First, you should know how to pick wild flowers," said Miss Parker. "That is very important. Not all children know how to pick wild flowers."

This is what Miss Parker wrote on the board:

How to Pick Wild Flowers
Do not pull up the flowers by their roots.
Pick only a few flowers of each kind.
Some wild flowers should never be picked.

"Now I will write the names of the wild flowers you have found." These are the names Miss Parker wrote:

Violet	Hepatica
Spring beauty	Bloodroot
Trillium	Jack-in-the-Pulpit

These are the things Miss Parker told the children about the wild flowers.

"You all know violets. But do you know that not all violets are violet color? Some violets are blue, some are white, some are yellow, and some are deep purple. The ones with the darkest and prettiest color grow in the shade. Because violets grow easily, you may pick many of them.

"Spring beauties are such dear little pink and white flowers. But see what thick stems they have and what thick, narrow leaves! Spring beauties grow in

the woods, too, but they live in dry places. If you see a great many spring beauties, you may pick some of them. But you should not waste them.

"This is a trillium. It has three leaves and three white petals. The trillium grows from a bulb. Just one flower grows from each bulb. If you pick the flower, you kill the plant. Let's not pick any more trilliums.

"These are hepaticas. They bloom almost before the snow has gone. Sometimes they bloom under dead leaves. I saw them blooming in the woods. They were like a blue carpet on the ground. Look at the soft hairs on the hepaticas.

"This is bloodroot. What a queer name for a flower with such white petals! This is how it got its name. The root has a red juice in it. The Indians used the juice for medicine. You should not pick many bloodroots. Their petals drop off very soon after the flower is picked.

"And this is Jack-in-the-pulpit! 'Jack' is the yellow center of the flower. It is really made of many yellow flowers growing on a large stem. A green part is wrapped around this large stem. You should not pick many Jack-in-the-pulpits for just one flower grows from each bulb."

"How much more interesting flowers are when we know their names!" said Susan.

The Red-Winged Blackbird

Have you seen a red-winged blackbird? Of course, you have. The male red-winged blackbird is a very pretty bird. He has very black feathers. On his shoulders are patches of red and yellow. The male is larger than the female. The female's feathers are brown and white. She is not bright. She is hard to see. Of course, she is safer because she is hard to see. Almost everyone knows the male red-winged blackbird, but very few know the female.

The male red-winged blackbirds come from the south early in spring. They come in large flocks. They fly to marshes. A marsh is wet ground. A marsh is near a river or lake or pond. Cat-tails grow in marshes. Cat-tails are weeds that grow in water. They grow tall. They have hollow stems.

The red-winged blackbirds sit on cat-tails in the marsh and sing. They wait for the females to come from the south.

And then such singing and calling and chattering you never heard! The males are choosing their mates.

After that is done, the females build nests. The red-winged blackbird's nest is deep. It must be deep to keep the eggs and babies from falling into the water. The nest is often made of cat-tail leaves. The leaves are woven together. The nest is sometimes fastened to cat-tails. It hangs between them.

In about twelve days the eggs hatch. At first the baby birds have no feathers. But as the birds grow, their feathers grow. Their parents feed them worms and caterpillars. The birds grow very fast. They can fly away from their nest in about ten days.

The young male blackbird looks like his mother. He does not have red and yellow feathers on his wings. The colored feathers do not grow until he is about a year old.

The male red-winged blackbird has a sharp call, but he sings a song which is very sweet. His song sounds happy and cheerful as it comes across the marsh.

Many red-winged blackbirds live together in a marsh. Flocks of blackbirds often fly together. They build their nests close together.

The red-winged blackbirds and the orioles belong to the same family of birds. They belong to the blackbird family.

Red-winged blackbirds eat insects that are harmful. Sometimes they eat the farmer's wheat. How angry the farmer is then! He does not think of all the good things the red-winged blackbirds do. He forgets that they eat many, many insects. Insects often destroy the farmer's crops.

Red-winged blackbirds, then, you see, are very useful birds. Besides, isn't it fun to see them sitting on the tall weeds?

wrong!

Ted Receives a Health Letter

Dear Ted,

I'm on a train. I'm going to the country with my uncle.

There are many people on this train. Some of them do not care very much about health. I saw a little girl eating an apple. She bought it from a boy on the train. She ate it without washing or peeling it.

A boy near me is writing a letter, too. But he puts his pencil into his mouth. He should know better than that.

Some people just went into the dining car for dinner. They did not wash their hands. I know their hands must be dirty. They have been on the train all morning.

Oh, my! The boy right in front of me used his brother's handkerchief to blow his nose. He has a bad cold. Now his brother may get the cold, too!

I wish that girl would stop biting her fingernails. She should know it is bad. It makes her nails look bad. And she shouldn't put her fingers into her mouth. I'd like to tell her about it. But I think I won't.

I met a boy on the train. He smiled at me. I like him, but he doesn't know much about health. His teeth need fixing. He ate a whole box of candy this morning. Then he didn't want any dinner.

My uncle says health is important. He says it is fine to know so much about health. He says that I am making a good record.

I like riding on the train. I am taking good care of myself. I am going to dinner now. I am hungry. I haven't had anything since breakfast. I'm sorry for those people who haven't learned about health. Some one should tell them.

Good-bye,

Charles

Getting Wool From Sheep

Cowboy Hal said, "Jack, do you want to watch us shear sheep today?"

Every spring men came to the ranch to shear the sheep. But this was the first time that Jack had been asked to watch.

"Yes, I want to watch," Jack said. "But why do we shear sheep every spring?"

"The sheep's wool would be too hot in summer," said Cowboy Hal. "And so we cut the wool off. You see, wool keeps the heat in the sheep's body. You wear woolen clothing in winter to keep you warm. The wool keeps in the heat. The wool on the sheep does the same thing. It keeps in the heat. When summer comes, you don't need wool clothing. You'd be too hot. So you take it off. Sheep don't need wool in the summer. They would be too hot. So we take their wool off. We shear them."

"Does it hurt the sheep?" asked Jack.

"Not any more than it hurts you to have your hair cut," laughed Cowboy Hal.

Jack and Cowboy Hal rode out to the sheep sheds. The men were shearing sheep in the sheds.

The men who were shearing the sheep used electric shears. Each man held a sheep between his legs. The sheep couldn't get away from him. He ran the shears up and down and around the sheep's back.

The wool was all off in a minute. The man threw the sheep's wool to one side and began to shear another sheep.

The wool from one sheep is called a *fleece*. Another man picked up each fleece. He tied it with string. He threw the fleece to a third man. This man stood by a big bag. He packed the fleeces into the bag. When the bag was full, it was much higher than Cowboy Hal.

Then the bag was fastened together at the top and put on a truck. There were many bags of wool on the truck. A man drove the truck to a train. The bags of wool were sent away. They went to a place where the wool could be made into warm clothes for winter.

The sheep looked bare and white after they were sheared. They were then put into a big tub of water. The water had medicine in it. The medicine killed the insects that lived on the sheep.

The sheep looked brown when they came out of the water. Then a man put a spot of paint on each sheep. This was called *branding* the sheep. It was the way Jack's father had of knowing his sheep. The paint would stay on until the sheep were sheared next spring.

After the sheep were branded with paint, they were taken up into the mountains. They would eat the green grass in the mountains all summer.

Jack's Bath

Jack came home from sheep shearing a very dirty boy. Jack took a bath. He could not think of eating supper while he was dirty. Jack did not have a nice bathroom. He could not turn on the hot and cold water. Jack brought a big tin tub into the kitchen. He filled it with warm water and took his bath in it.

Jack knew how to take a bath. He used warm water and lots of soap. He washed his neck and ears. He washed his whole body with soap. He dried himself with a big soft towel. He put on clean clothes. Then he was ready for supper.

In summer Jack gets hot and dirty. He takes a bath every night.

A Friend of the Farmer

One day Jack was walking through the meadow. He was going after the cows. Suddenly he heard the clear call of a bird.

"A meadowlark!" he said. "You-oo-oo can't see me! That's what you say, Meadowlark! But I *can* see you! You're sitting right over there on that fence. You have yellow feathers on your breast. And around your throat you have a band of black. Yes, sir. I *can* see you. I can see you very well."

A bird flew into the air. It almost flew into Jack's face. Jack jumped and almost fell. "Oh!" he cried. "I almost stepped on a nest!"

There on the ground was a nest. It was almost hidden in the weeds.

"It must be a meadowlark's nest!" cried Jack. "That was a meadowlark that flew away and almost hit me. Let's see!"

Jack pushed away the grass so that he could see the nest better. The nest was made of dry grass. It was lined with horse hairs. Over the top of it was a roof. The roof was made of grass. The roof almost hid the eggs inside the nest.

"The meadowlark hides her nest well," said Jack. "I don't believe even Cowboy Hal could have found this one."

There were four eggs in the nest. They were larger than robin's eggs. And they were speckled. The mother meadowlark sits on the eggs all day and all night. She leaves only when she wants something to eat. Of course she leaves her nest when a young cowboy almost steps on her!

The meadowlark that Jack saw was the western meadowlark. It lives in the western part of the United States. It has a beautiful clear song.

There is a meadowlark that lives in the eastern part of the United States. It looks like the one Jack saw. But it does not sing the same song.

Many people have tried to put the song of the meadowlark into words. Some people think the meadowlark says:

"I see you-oo-oo.
"You ca-a-an't see me-e-e-e."

Other people think the meadowlark says:

"Spring of the ye-e-ear!"

Whatever the meadowlark says, it has a song that every one remembers. It is one of the prettiest and sweetest of bird songs.

The meadowlark belongs to the same family as the red-winged blackbird. But it is quite different. The red-winged blackbird usually makes its nest in cattails. The meadowlark makes its nest on the ground. Their songs are very different, too. And, of course, they do not look alike. Their beaks are alike.

The meadowlarks are great friends of the farmer. They eat insects that eat plants. Farmers are glad when meadowlarks come to their field. They help save the farmer's crops.

A Spring Shower

It was raining. How the drops beat on the windows! How the water ran down the sidewalks!

Suddenly there came a flash of lightning and a clap of thunder.

"What makes lightning?" asked Dick.

"Electricity," said Miss Parker.

"Electricity like electric lights?" asked Dick.

"Not just like electric lights," said Miss Parker. "Did you ever rub a cat's back and make a spark?"

"Yes," said Dick.

"That was electricity. Did your hair ever snap when you combed it?" asked Miss Parker.

"My hair has done that," said Susan.

"That is electricity, too. There is electricity in the air. Sometimes you feel it when you walk on a carpet and then touch some one," said Miss Parker.

"Oh, I know," said Jimmy. "You get a shock. Sometimes you see a spark."

"Lightning is something like that," said Miss Parker. "It's a big spark of electricity that jumps through the air."

While Miss Parker was talking, the sun came out.

"Oh, there is a rainbow!" cried Nancy.

The children ran to the windows. The rainbow grew brighter and brighter.

"Isn't it beautiful!" said Susan. "What makes a rainbow?"

"The sunlight makes a rainbow," said Miss Parker.

"But the rainbow has colors in it," said Dick. "Sunlight doesn't have colors."

"But sunlight does have colors. It has all colors in it," said Miss Parker.

The children were surprised.

"I'll show you," said Miss Parker.

She went to the cupboard and got a piece of glass. It looked like a crystal. It was shaped like this.

Miss Parker pulled down the window shade until just a beam of sunlight came through it. The beam shone on the blackboard.

"What color is the light on the board?" she asked.

"White," the children said.

Then Miss Parker held the piece of glass in the beam of light.

"Oh, there's a rainbow!" cried Jane.

"It isn't the shape of a rainbow," said Dick.

"No," said Miss Parker. "And it isn't a rainbow. Rainbows are made when the sun shines through rain. The colors you see are made when the sun shines through this glass."

"What makes the colors?" asked Bob.

"Sunlight has all the rainbow colors in it," Miss Parker told them. "When you see them all together they look white. But when the light shines through this piece of glass, you can see each color."

She wrote the colors on the board.

violet
indigo
blue
green
yellow
orange
red

"May we hold the glass and make some colors?" asked Susan.

"Yes," said Miss Parker.

She brought out several of the glass pieces. The children made colors on the blackboard. They could always see the colors of the rainbow.

Miss Parker told the children that raindrops break up sunlight into its colors.

"Have you seen rainbows in other places than the sky?" she asked.

"I saw a rainbow in the water when Dad watered the grass," Bob said.

"That's right," said Miss Parker. "Watch for places where the sunlight is making colors."

The children had fun with their rainbows. They named the colors and wrote them on the board. Miss Parker gave them pieces of paper in rainbow colors. They made paper rainbows to take home with them.

"We get heat and light from the sun," said Jane. "We get rainbows, too."

How Well Do You Remember?

1. What makes the milk come up this straw?

2. What do we call a butterfly when it looks like this?

3. What is this rock picture called?

4. What kind of food does this bird eat?

5. How old is this twig?

6. What makes the sound in this toy?

7. What do we call a place where small land animals may be kept?

8. What is this animal doing?

Off to Camp

Ted was going to camp. He was excited. It was his first trip to camp. He was only eight.

The camp belonged to Mr. Page. Ted lived in a big city. Mr. Page's camp was in the country. It was a good place for boys. They learned many things at camp that boys should know.

Ted packed many things to take with him. He left early one morning on a train. He had never been on a train before. He arrived at the camp about noon. Some boys met the train. They were glad to see Ted. Ted liked the boys. He was sure he would like the camp.

Many of the boys had never been to camp. Most of them were older than Ted. Some of them had been sick. They needed good food, fresh air, and sunshine.

How hungry Ted was! He was glad it was time for dinner. And what a dinner it was! All kinds of food that boys need to make them strong and well!

There were many things to do at the camp. The boys were busy all day. There was a boat to row, there were fish to catch, and there were trails for hikes.

In the evening the boys sat about the campfire. They told stories. When they had finished their stories, Mr. Page said, "You will like this camp if you do your part. Each boy must take care of his own tent. He must also take care of his body. We must get well and strong in camp. We must learn to help each other."

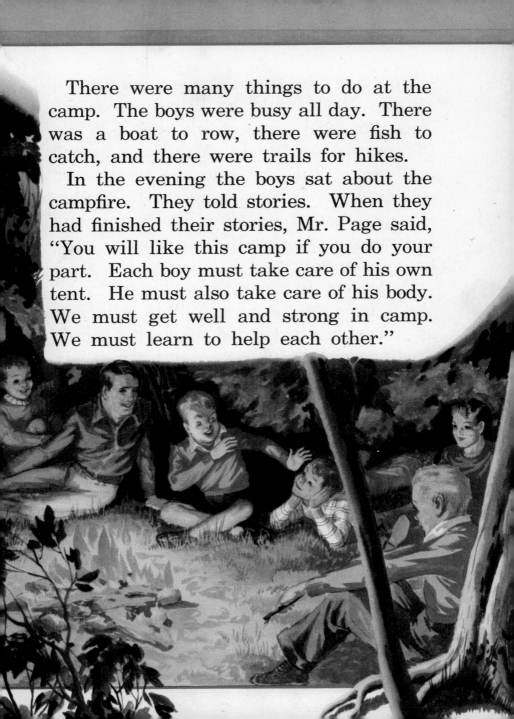

Next morning the boys were up at seven o'clock. They could smell bacon cooking. Each boy took care of his tent. When the tents were ready, Mr. Page looked at them. When he said the tents were all right, everybody went to breakfast. Oranges, cereal, toast, milk, bacon, and eggs were soon eaten. The boys were ready for a busy day.

"It is very important to eat good food," Mr. Page told the boys. "But it is just as important to get rid of waste. Some waste comes through your skin when you sweat. Most of the waste must come through your bowels. So don't forget bowel movements at least once each day. Right after breakfast is a good time to remember this rule."

After breakfast the boys ran down to the lake. They were going fishing. But the big boat was too heavy to lift. When Mr. Page came, he said, "Let's try a lever on it."

"What is a lever?" asked the boys.

"I'll show you," said Mr. Page.

He got a long pole. He put one end under the boat. He put a piece of log under the pole near the boat.

Then the boys pushed down on the pole. Up came the boat. It slid into the lake. The boys were excited.

"A lever helps do work," said Ted.

"Yes," said Mr. Page. "A lever is a machine. It will help you do many things."

The boys caught enough fish for dinner. What fun they had eating the fish they had caught!

After dinner each boy rested.

"A rest after dinner is good for you," said Mr. Page.

In the afternoon the boys went for a hike. Mr. Page went with them. When they got back to camp, they were ready for swims and baths. Each boy used lots of soap and water to get clean.

"You must take care of your bodies. You must keep them clean," said Mr. Page. "Your head gets dirty, too. If you want to be clean, you must wash your hair. Then the oil can come through your skin and keep your skin and hair soft.

"You must take good care of your fingernails, too. You must not let them get too long. You must keep them clean. You must also remember not to bite your fingernails."

Ted made a list of health rules.   He put at the top of his list:

Rules for Ted, Made by Ted

1. Keep your tent clean.
2. Hang up your clothes.
3. Wash your hands and face.
   Brush your hair and teeth.
4. Remember bowel movements
       right after breakfast.
   Then wash your hands.
5. Take care of your nails.
   Never bite them.
6. Take a bath every day.
   Use warm water.
   Use a wash cloth.
   Use soap.
7. Keep your hair clean.
8. Rest after dinner.
9. Go to bed at eight o'clock.

Ted showed his rules to Mr. Page.

"They are good rules," said Mr. Page. "They will keep you well and strong."

The next day the boys rowed their boat across the lake. Then they hiked up to an old mill. The old mill was on a river. A long time ago farmers brought their corn to this mill. The corn was ground into meal. It was ground between two big stones. A big water wheel made the stones grind. The water wheel was still in the river. The water made it go around. "This is a way to make water do work," said Mr. Page.

On their way back to the boat, the boys moved a big rock from the road. They used a lever to move it. They found a pole and moved the rock just as they had moved the boat.

They learned about other kinds of levers. They learned that all these machines are levers.

The boys were sorry when camp was over. The last night at camp they talked about many of the things they had done.

"I am glad we learned about machines," said Ted. "Machines help us do work. Yesterday we saw another water wheel. A water wheel is a machine. It was working. It was making electricity. The man who runs it told us about it. He said it made the electricity for this camp. We saw a windmill, too. It was working. It was pumping water for a farmer's cattle."